LEADERS OF THE CIVIL WAR ERA

Stonewall Jackson

LEADERS OF THE CIVIL WAR ERA

John Brown

Jefferson Davis

Frederick Douglass

Ulysses S. Grant

Stonewall Jackson

Robert E. Lee

Abraham Lincoln

William Tecumseh Sherman

Harriet Beecher Stowe

Harriet Tubman

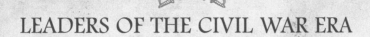

LEADERS OF THE CIVIL WAR ERA

Stonewall Jackson

Rachel A. Koestler-Grack

CHELSEA HOUSE
PUBLISHERS
An imprint of Infobase Publishing

STONEWALL JACKSON

Copyright © 2009 by Infobase Publishing
All rights reserved. No part of this book may be reproduced or utilized in any form or by any means, electronic or mechanical, including photocopying, recording, or by any information storage or retrieval systems, without permission in writing from the publisher. For information contact:

Chelsea House
An imprint of Infobase Publishing
132 West 31st Street
New York NY 10001

Library of Congress Cataloging-in-Publication Data
Koestler-Grack, Rachel A., 1973-
  Stonewall Jackson / by Rachel Koestler-Grack.
    p. cm. — (Leaders of the Civil War era)
  Includes bibliographical references and index.
  ISBN 978-1-60413-299-1 (hardcover)
  1. Jackson, Stonewall, 1824-1863—Juvenile literature. 2. Generals—United States—Biography—Juvenile literature. 3. Generals—Confederate States of America—Biography—Juvenile literature. 4. United States. Army—Biography--Juvenile literature. 5. Confederate States of America. Army—Biography—Juvenile literature. 6. United States—History—Civil War, 1861-1865—Biography—Juvenile literature. I. Title. II. Series.

E467.1.J15K64 2009
973.7'3092—dc22
  [B]   2008044611

Chelsea House books are available at special discounts when purchased in bulk quantities for businesses, associations, institutions, or sales promotions. Please call our Special Sales Department in New York at (212) 967-8800 or (800) 322-8755.

You can find Chelsea House on the World Wide Web at http://www.chelseahouse.com
Series design by Erik Lindstrom
Cover design by Keith Trego

Printed in the United States of America

Bang FOF 10 9 8 7 6 5 4 3 2 1

This book is printed on acid-free paper.

All links and Web addresses were checked and verified to be correct at the time of publication. Because of the dynamic nature of the Web, some addresses and links may have changed since publication and may no longer be valid.

⚔ CONTENTS ⚔

1 "Rally, Brave Men, and Press Forward!" 7

2 Orphan Boy 14

3 West Point Cadet 23

4 The Mexican War 34

5 The Lexington Years 55

6 War 72

7 Seven Days 99

8 "Let Us Cross Over the River" 114

Chronology and Timeline 122

Glossary 126

Bibliography 128

Further Resources 129

Picture Credits 131

Index 132

About the Author 136

"Rally, Brave Men, and Press Forward!"

In 1862, Major General John Pope faced nothing but trouble in Virginia. President Abraham Lincoln had put him in charge of the revamped Army of Virginia. The 40-year-old Union general was quick tempered, brash, and rude. His own soldiers despised him. Pope bragged that, in battle, he had seen only the backs of his enemy. As his forces swept through Virginia, across the Rappahannock River toward Charlottesville, he instructed his soldiers to loot and plunder Confederate towns. He forced Southerners living within his lines to swear an oath of allegiance to the Union. If they broke their pledge, he shot them without a second thought.

When stories about this Union thug trickled into Stonewall Jackson's camp, one of his men said, "This new general claims your attention."

At the young soldier's words, the Confederate general did not break his gaze. Oftentimes, when Jackson was deep in thought, he stared off into the distance. His steely blue eyes were focused somewhere in rolling clouds. The soldier was right. Pope was begging for Jackson's attention, almost taunting him. "He shall have it," Jackson said, as quoted in *Stonewall Jackson*, by Donald Davis.

Pope had anchored his army around the town of Culpeper and had spread flanking divisions off to Fredericksburg, to the east, and faraway Sperryville, to the west. Immediately, Jackson spotted a weakness in Pope's army. When the Union force at Culpeper advanced, it was too far forward. It was exposed and was out of reach of a quick rescue from either flank. If Jackson crushed the middle division, the Union's Army of Virginia would be divided. Jackson would deal with the flanks later.

Much to Jackson's delight, he found out that the central force was commanded by an old foe—Nathaniel Banks. Banks had chased Jackson all over the Shenandoah Valley. At each encounter, Jackson had outsmarted the Union general. "He is always ready to fight, and he generally gets whipped," Jackson joked. On August 7, 1862, Jackson's 18,000 Confederate soldiers began a daylong march, beneath a scorching summer sun, from Gordonsville to Orange Court House in Virginia's Orange County. From this point, they would continue to Culpeper, 20 miles away.

Rarely did Jackson tell his division commanders of his plans. This time, however, on the advice of General Robert E. Lee, he made an exception. Jackson's orders were very clear. One Confederate division, commanded by Richard Ewell, would take the lead. General A.P. Hill, commanding the light artillery division, would follow. Charles Sidney Winder, who had been too sick even to mount his horse, would bring up the rear.

On Saturday morning, August 9, the Confederates began their march to Culpeper. Around noon, Jackson's lead divisions, covered in a fine white dust, forded the Rapidan River

General Stonewall Jackson was one of the most prominent military figures during the Civil War. A decorated war hero, Jackson's military experience made him a courageous warrior for the Confederacy, and his victories against Union forces transformed him into a legendary figure.

and moved in on the Yankees. One of the Confederates spotted Union soldiers on a ridge straight ahead. Jackson spurred his faithful horse, Little Sorrel, and tore off, charging a bit too fast. Jackson, always hungry for battle, started the fight before all of his troops were there.

Union forces had set up on Cedar Mountain, a good position for waging battle. Jackson sent a division ahead, and the Confederates drove the Yankees off the mountain with surprising ease. Ewell secured the high ground, thereby giving Jackson a stable artillery position. The Confederates unleashed their big guns on Union forces on a distant ridge. This triggered a two-hour duel between the Rebels, who had more guns, and the Yankees, who had bigger ones. A Union shot struck and killed General Winder, who had been commanding Jackson's legendary Stonewall Brigade. Brigadier General William Taliaferro took over.

Union general Banks charged the center of the Confederate line with two infantry brigades that he had hidden in the cornfield of a nearby farm. Ignoring the rain of musket shot and blasting cannon fire, Jackson galloped Little Sorrel into the heat of battle. At one point, he ordered his staff to retreat while he stayed behind. He argued that the Yankees would not waste a shot on a single horseman. Moments later, a cannonball blew a nearby tree to splinters. All the while, Jackson's mind was taking pictures of the battle. He was calmly evaluating the situation so that he could effectively direct his unit. Few generals had ever led on the front line as Stonewall Jackson did. He was confident, composed, and fearless, and he trusted that he would die only when God wanted him to die.

At last, Jackson decided that most of the Union strength was on the right side of the road, where the Confederates had a firm anchor on the mountain. As Jackson moved his men into position, another brigade of Yankee infantry suddenly dashed out of a wheat field on the other side of the road. The Yankees slammed into the Rebel line, which was not yet secure. Several

Confederate brigades broke. Unable to tolerate the sight of his men running away like frightened rabbits, Jackson pulled out his sword and waved it over his head. "Rally, brave men, and press forward!" he cried. "Your general will lead you! Jackson will lead you! Follow me!" He grabbed a Confederate battle flag and charged forward, with the flag flapping behind him in the breeze. Bullets were flying and soldiers were falling, but inspired by their brave general, Jackson's men turned on the Yankees. In a final, fierce rush, they trampled the enemy.

By sunset, the Battle of Cedar Mountain was over. Jackson refused to settle for a simple victory, however. He believed in a merciless, total war. Besides, Pope had it coming. Jackson pushed forward into the night. By the blue glow of the moon, Rebel soldiers pursued the fleeing Yankees until they could chase no more.

A LEGEND

Stonewall Jackson stepped into the limelight during the most tumultuous period of American history—the Civil War. During this time, ordinary men became mythical war heroes. Gifted with the very genius of war, Jackson became one of the Civil War's leading actors, and the battlefield was his glorious stage. Seeming to be in a hundred places at once, he defeated three separate Union armies that outnumbered him two to one. He was feared by Union soldiers. Any army that faced Jackson made certain that it was manned to the fullest.

Jackson was respected and admired by his men, especially his famous Stonewall Brigade. With his gruff, unkempt appearance, he looked more like a common soldier than a general. This helped him to form a tight bond with his men, the most important relationship that can be formed in warfare. Time and time again, Jackson asked his men to do the impossible. Yet, despite the odds, his army had one success after another. His men trusted him implicitly and believed that, with Stonewall leading them, there was no way they could lose.

Commanding a regiment known as the Stonewall Brigade *(above)*, Jackson implemented rigorous training and discipline on his men. His ability to earn the absolute loyalty and respect of his troops helped spur them on to victories against the Union, furthering Jackson's mythical reputation. The Stonewall Brigade was so successful and effective, writers have often compared it to some of the greatest battle units in history.

Jackson's humble beginnings as an orphan boy taught him how to survive and to persevere, no matter what the circumstances. His unwavering grit brought him up through the ranks at the United States Military Academy at West Point and set him apart as a soldier in the Mexican War. Never defeated in any of his major battles, Jackson became a legend in his own time. His untimely death only added to his epic reputation. His dying embedded all the might-have-beens in the collective imagination.

Orphan Boy

A blustery wind beat at the door of Jonathan and Julia Jackson's brick house in Clarksburg, Virginia. The sun had long since dipped behind the Allegheny Mountains, and Julia had been in labor all evening. As the night ticked on, the hours seemed to melt together under the thick, black sky. In the early morning hours on January 20, 1824, Julia gave birth to her third son, Thomas.

Thomas's great-grandfather John Jackson had been born in Ireland to parents of English ancestry. John Jackson immigrated to America in 1748. On the ship, he met his future wife, Elizabeth Cummins of London. The couple settled in Maryland, where they raised their eight children. After 20 years, the family moved to rural Virginia and later made the trek across the Allegheny Mountains to the rugged frontier wilderness of northwestern Virginia. John found a clearing of land near the Buckhannon River. To claim the land as his own, he drove his tomahawk into a tree at the edge of the clearing.

John and Elizabeth Jackson's second son, Edward, worked his way up to the rank of colonel in the American army in the Revolutionary War. After the war, Edward made a small fortune in real estate. He married twice and fathered 15 children, the third of whom was Jonathan. As the son of a wealthy family, Jonathan Jackson had the best possible education. He became a lawyer. His family name opened up numerous opportunities for him, but he failed to take advantage of them. Instead, he squandered a sizeable inheritance on gambling and risky business schemes. In the end, he lost his land and most of his belongings, except for his slaves.

Although he was quite a scoundrel, Jonathan, with his flashing blue eyes, was charming. He won the affection of Julia Neale. The couple married in 1817. Marriage did not change Jackson's lifestyle, however. He continued to borrow money and pledged almost everything in his family's three-bedroom house, from the butter churn to the bed, as collateral. In 1819, Jonathan and Julia had their first child, a girl whom they named Elizabeth. Two years later, Julia gave birth to her first son, Warren. Thomas followed in the winter of 1824.

When Thomas was two years old, his six-year-old sister contracted typhoid fever. At about the same time, his father also became ill with this deadly disease. Within a month, little Elizabeth died. Shortly after, Jonathan followed. The day after her husband's death, Julia Jackson gave birth to another daughter, Laura Ann.

Because of Jonathan's debts, the family was left nearly penniless. To support her children, Julia took on odd jobs sewing and mending and also began teaching. Before long, Julia met a Clarksburg, Virginia, lawyer named Blake Woodson. They married in 1830 and moved the family to nearby Fayette

County. Soon after, Julia became pregnant again. Because Julia and Blake Woodson's finances were as frail as Jonathan Jackson's had been, the couple worried that they would be unable to support all of the children. Julia made the heart-wrenching decision to send her three children to live with relatives. Ten-year-old Warren went to live with Julia's brother in Ohio. Thomas and Laura moved in with Jonathan's brother Cummins at nearby Jackson's Mill.

Within a few months, all three children were rushed back to their mother's side. During the birth of her last son, Wirt, Julia had suffered serious complications. The children sat on the bed and nestled near their mother as they whispered their tearful good-byes. In the short span of five years, Thomas Jackson had lost both his parents. He now was a seven-year-old orphan boy, scared and unsure of his future.

LIFE AT JACKSON'S MILL

Thomas's uncle Cummins stood a burly six feet, two inches tall. He could lift a whiskey barrel straight up to his face, pull the cork out with his teeth, and suck a mouthful as easily as most men could drink from a cup. To a young boy longing for a father figure, Cummins Jackson's muscular arms glistened like those of a hero. Thomas took an instant liking to his uncle, who gave Thomas and Laura Ann a picture-perfect home in his house beside a rumbling river. Nearby, the whining of the sawmill droned on for hours as logs were sliced, chopped, and chewed. On some days, Thomas helped his uncle work at the mill or in the fields. Cummins trained Thomas as a horse jockey, and he rode in races on his uncle's own four-mile track. Although he wasn't smothered with hugs and kisses, Thomas felt comfortable in his adopted home.

One afternoon, Thomas got some shocking news. He and Laura were being sent to live with an aunt in Parkersburg. Ten-year-old Thomas would have no part of it. Stubborn and determined, he marched out of his aunt's home and walked all

Orphaned at a young age, General Stonewall Jackson found a stable home with relatives at Jackson's Mill in Virginia *(above)*. The mill, which was founded by Jackson's grandparents, fostered a sense of honesty, hard work, and responsibility in Jackson. Under the supervision of his Uncle Cummins, the young boy became involved in the family traditions of milling and regional politics.

the way back to Jackson's Mill. The Jacksons welcomed Thomas back into their home and never tried to send him away again.

At Jackson's Mill, Thomas learned how to be a tough, hard worker. On some days, however, he used his leisure time to turn a little profit. Like most young boys, he liked to fish, and he found a buyer for his catches, a man named Conrad Kester. Each time he toted his pole to the creek, he'd come back with a few fish to sell. One sunny afternoon, Colonel Talbott stopped Thomas on his way to Kester's. Dangling from Thomas's shoulder was a big pike. Colonel Talbott called up the road, "Why, if it's not young Tom Jackson. What do you have over your shoulder there?"

As quoted in *Stonewall Jackson* by John Bowers, Thomas replied, "It's a pike, sir."

"Give you a dollar for it, Tom," Talbott offered.

"Can't, sir. This one has already been sold."

"Well, now, I'll give you a dollar and a quarter," Talbott bargained. "No one's going to give you more than that."

Undoubtedly, the offer was tempting. Thomas was determined to be fair and honest to his regular customer, however. "No, sir, I can't do that, Colonel Talbott," he said. "I've promised Conrad Kester to him all the fish I catch at fifty cents each. He's taken them much smaller. It wouldn't be right to deny him now that a big one has come along." With that, Thomas picked up his pace and headed straight for Conrad Kester's house.

At 17, Thomas took his first serious job. He served in nearby Weston as Lewis County constable, carrying out the duties of a deputy sheriff. Through this work, he met Colonel Alexander Scott Withers, a teacher in a private school located in the courthouse. Colonel Withers was also a justice of the peace and an authority on frontier history. He was the author of *Chronicles of Border Warfare*, the first book to be printed west of the Allegheny Mountains. Withers sensed that Thomas was special and had extraordinary potential. One day, while Thomas was making his rounds, he noticed the colonel at the mill, buying a sack of meal. Thomas hurried over and offered to deliver the sack to the colonel's home. "We have servants for that," Withers replied. "If you work with your head you don't have to work with your hands."

Thomas took the colonel's words to heart. Growing up on the frontier, he had had little opportunity for a good education. Only wealthy children could afford decent schooling. Still, somehow, Thomas knew that he was destined for more than just a life of farming. In early 1842, Thomas found out that the district's congressman, Representative Samuel Lewis Hays, was coming to Weston. He was coming to offer one young man a free university education: an appointment to the United States Military Academy at West Point, New York. Thomas was determined to win that scholarship. He knew that he would be at a disadvantage compared with other applicants. He lacked a formal education and had learned only the basics—reading and writing—in his sporadic school-days. Representative Hays probably was looking for someone familiar with mathematics and engineering, important sub-jects for an aspiring military officer. Thomas wasn't going to be discouraged by such obstacles, however. In one interview, as recorded in Donald Davis's *Stonewall Jackson*, he admitted, "I am very ignorant. But I know I have the energy and I think I have the intellect."

As it turned out, Thomas was one of four applicants. One of the four was turned away because he was too young, which left just three. The two other contenders were Thomas's friends; one of them, Gibson Butcher, was a young man who worked as a clerk for the county. The competitive examination was administered by Captain George Washington Jackson, a distant relative of Thomas's. As a professional, Captain Jackson remained neutral. Gibson Butcher, the courthouse clerk, was granted the scholarship. Nimble with numbers, he earned the top score. When he arrived at West Point, however, he was overwhelmed by the rigorous discipline and harsh treatment of the cadets. On June 4, 1842, he left the academy without even informing Congressman Hays.

On his way home, Butcher stopped at Jackson's Mill and told Thomas of his decision. The original group of appli-cants had now dwindled to two, Thomas and his friend Joe Lightburn. This time around, Cummins Jackson decided to throw around some Jackson weight. He launched a campaign to get Thomas selected. Numerous family members wrote let-ters of recommendation, and signatures were gathered from people who knew the congressman. Among the signatures was that of Representative Hays's own son, another good friend of Thomas's.

Cummins dashed to Washington to hand Hays Butcher's resignation papers along with a thick bundle of documents recommending Thomas for the open slot. The boy may have lacked formal education, but his steely determination went

WEST POINT: THE UNITED STATES MILITARY ACADEMY

As the oldest continuously occupied military post in America, West Point's role in U.S. history dates back to the Revolutionary War. General George Washington considered the commanding plateau on the west bank of the Hudson River the most important strategic position in America. In 1778, Washington personally selected Thaddeus Kosciuszko, one of the heroes of the Battle of Saratoga, to design the fortifications for West Point. By 1779, Washington had transferred his headquarters to the West Point fortress. American soldiers built the fortress's forts, batteries, and redoubts. They also draped an iron chain weighing 150 tons across the Hudson to control river traffic. Fortress West Point was never captured by the British during the war.

In 1802, President Thomas Jefferson signed legislation that established the United States Military Academy (USMA) at West Point. Colonel Sylvanus Thayer, the superintendent of West Point from 1817 to 1833, is known as the "Father of the Academy." He upgraded academic standards, instilled military discipline, and emphasized the importance of hon-

unmatched. On June 17, Thomas was admitted as a cadet at the United States Military Academy.

Before he left for West Point, Thomas met with the secretary of war, John Canfield Spencer, who gave him an inkling of what to expect from the other students. Most of them were wealthy, upper-class young men with excellent educations. Coming

orable conduct. Aware of the nation's need for engineers, Thayer made civil engineering the foundation of the West Point curriculum. For the first 50 years of the school's existence, graduates of the USMA were largely responsible for the design and construction of the country's railway lines, bridges, harbors, and roads.

During the Mexican War and the Indian Wars, West Point graduates gained valuable experience and national recognition. During the American Civil War (1861–1865), West Pointers dominated the highest ranks of the armies of both sides. Such graduates as Ulysses S. Grant, Robert E. Lee, William T. Sherman, and Stonewall Jackson set high standards of military leadership in both the North and the South.

Now more than 200 years old, the United States Military Academy at West Point continues to ensure that all of its programs and policies support the needs of the army and the nation today and into the future. The academy, with its long and noble history, remains a revered institution that attracts some of the best and brightest young men and women in America. Today, West Point offers a challenging array of opportunities as it maintains its traditional commitment to Duty, Honor, and Country.

from the rough-and-tumble frontier wilderness, Thomas might not be accepted by the other cadets. As recounted in Davis's biography, the secretary of war offered Thomas this bit of advice: "Sir, you have a good name. Go to West Point, and the first man who insults you, knock him down, and have it charged to my account!"

West Point Cadet

Thomas arrived at West Point in June of 1842. He was part of the largest entering class at that time, with a total of 123 young cadets. After the first exams, however, 30 of the cadets were dismissed, and the number dwindled further as the year wore on. Most of the cadets were under 18 years of age. One of them—George B. McClellan of Pennsylvania—was only 15 years old when he was accepted into the academy.

In the first week of July, the cadets started summer camp at Camp Spencer. They moved from the barracks onto the open plains. Jackson slept under a canvas tent and rose before the sun began to heat the inside of the tent. He nestled down at night directly on the grass. Everything at Camp Spencer was designed to be rough and hard to weed out any fainthearted cadets. The cadets' day started at five thirty in the morning and went on until sundown—a grueling routine of drilling, maneuvers, and long marches.

Cadets were expected to study a manual of arms that detailed every weapon in the military and offered instruction on guard duty, fatigue details, and parades. The cadets' equipment had to be ready for inspection around the clock. At all times and in all kinds of weather, their new uniforms of a gray coat, white pantaloons, and a round, box-style hat with pompon and spread eagle were to be spotless. The first-year students, or plebes, were at the mercy of their masters—the wolflike upperclassmen. These more senior cadets snapped and snarled out orders. Almost constantly, the first-year cadets ran errands for their seniors; they put up their tents and fetched them water. For many plebes, the hazing was much worse, however. West Point veterans hurled insults and ridiculed the freshmen at every opportunity.

At 18, Jackson was older than most of his fellow plebes, and the hazing hardly affected him. He had grown up around fiery and rowdy men who often pushed him to his physical limits. His rugged backwoods childhood already had instilled in him a solid base of survival and perseverance. The older cadets mocked him with the nickname "the general," because he had the same last name as former president Andrew Jackson—the famous general from the War of 1812. Instead of buckling under the taunts of the upper-classmen, he easily withstood their heckling. In late August, summer camp ended. Jackson had endured his first military test. Now, however, came his hardest challenge: the classroom.

As part of Company D, he and his classmates moved into the first floor of the North Barracks. A typical, two-person room was 12 feet square, with a rough pine floor, two iron-framed beds, and a desk and chair for each cadet. In the morning, cadets rolled up their mattresses and made sure that each article of clothing was hanging on the proper hook. Cadets were not allowed to hang pictures or decorations on the bare,

Raised in rural Virginia, Stonewall Jackson initially struggled when he started his cadetship at West Point. Although he was clever, Jackson was unfamiliar with the educational concepts being taught in his classes and struggled mightily to keep up with the other cadets. His determination to succeed, however, helped him overcome his obstacles and Jackson began to rise in the class ranks. *Above*, West Point cadets in uniform at the academy.

whitewashed walls. During the winter months, a drafty fireplace provided scanty warmth.

For six days a week, cadets followed the same monotonous schedule. At dawn, the drum rolls of reveille sounded, followed immediately by roll call. Thirty minutes later, the rooms were inspected. From that time until 7:00, cadets ate breakfast and studied. At 8:00, cadets reported for guard mounting, or changing of the guard, and recreation. Afterwards, the academic day began.

For five straight hours, students attended classes. From 1:00 to 2:00 in the afternoon, cadets grabbed lunch and had a little time for relaxation. After lunch, there were two more hours of classes. From 4:00 until sunset, the cadets spent time in drill, maneuvers, and parade. After taking an hour for supper, they retired to their rooms and studied. When the 9:30 tattoo sounded, cadets had one half hour to prepare for the next day and finish up their chores. At 10:00, the lights went out, and all cadets were supposed to be in bed. From reveille to tattoo, the cadets' day offered 10 hours of classroom work and study, three hours of military exercises, two-and-a-half hours of recreation, and two hours for meals. Cadets were under constant supervision, and even a moment of privacy was rare.

Although no cadet ever went hungry, meals were bland, with little variety. The usual meal was heavy on meat, potatoes, and bread. Vegetables, fruits, and sweets were added from time to time but not every day. Jackson paid little attention to the food, however. He was focused on his classroom studies, which were posing definite problems.

At the end of his first year at West Point, out of 72 cadets remaining in his class, Jackson finished seventeenth in French, forty-fifth in math, and fifty-first in general merit. He also racked up 15 demerits. Almost three-fourths of the course work at the academy was concentrated on mathematics, science, and engineering. Mathematics was the dominant subject. Cadets spent an hour and a half each day, six days a week, trying to master math concepts. Jackson's brilliant younger classmate George McClellan, who had two years of college behind him before he was admitted to West Point, admitted that he did not have to study much. Jackson, however, with his scant backwoods education, was ill prepared for complicated college courses. Even simple fractions stumped him. It seemed that no matter how hard he tried, he could not grasp the equations. In class, he stood at the blackboard and fiercely scraped out numbers in chalk as sweat beaded on his forehead. Classmates mocked, "Look out, the general's going to flood the place."

Jackson barely squeaked by on daily tests and quizzes, and his grades sank. Day after day, he trudged along with the other "immortals"—cadets whose rankings were so low that they were in jeopardy of being kicked out of the academy. If a cadet failed a course, he had to pack his bags and leave. Algebra, geometry, and other math courses accounted for 40 percent of cadet failures. Gibson Butcher had quit and returned home to Weston. Jackson did not want to bring further disappointment to the people of Weston or to his Uncle Cummins. He vowed that he "would go through or die." He had to come up with a plan to survive at West Point.

CLIMBING THE RANKS

Jackson refused to surrender. He attacked his studies with the same raw determination that would drive his military career. As his roommate slept, he huddled over the glowing embers of coal in the fireplace to study. On February 20, 1843, Jackson's plebe probationary period officially ended. He signed an oath of allegiance to the U.S. Army and became a full-fledged cadet. With his grades still lingering near failure, he decided, finally, to move at his own pace rather than to try to keep up with his classmates. He did not tackle a new problem until he had conquered the one before. He focused on his own method and did not worry about being docked for late assignments. By spring, his grades began to show slight improvement.

When he studied, Jackson seemed to be lost somewhere in his mind. He was so focused that he was unaware of anything else. Former roommate Parmenas Turnley, a cadet from Tennessee, commented in James Robertson's *Stonewall Jackson*, "No one I have ever known could so perfectly withdraw his mind from surrounding objects or influences." Jackson's goal was to absorb whatever he was reading so thoroughly that it would be as if he had written the words himself. Point by point, he pulled up his grades and, slowly and steadily, climbed the ranks at West Point. During that year, in 1843, future Union general Ulysses S. Grant observed Jackson to be "the most honest human being I ever knew—painfully conscientious, very slow in acquiring information, but a hard, incessant student." This strong-willed desire to succeed drove him to study as much as 16 hours a day.

By the end of his second year, Jackson's logical approach had served him well. He finished eighteenth in math, fifty-second in French, fifty-fifth in engineering, and thirteenth in general merit. He earned 26 demerits. He excelled in ethics and in a group of courses known as natural and experimental philosophy. These included physics, mechanics, and astronomy. In these subjects, which demanded logic, science, and reason, Jackson achieved his highest marks. He still struggled in some classes, however, such as French and drawing. French was required because many military and technical texts were written in that language. Drawing consisted of sketch work of subjects that ranged from human figures to topography and landscape designs. Skill at drawing was important in the field, where officers often had to draw up plans for military maneuvers and attacks. Jackson also had a difficult time with horsemanship, even though he had ridden often at his uncle's track. Back in Weston, Jackson had ridden workhorses—mounts that differed greatly from the thoroughbreds at West Point. In the saddle, Jackson resembled Washington Irving's fictional Ichabod Crane; he looked like an overgrown jockey with awkward riding posture.

Not only was Jackson trying to improve his academic standing; he also was working on shaping his character. He learned the social graces—how to engage in polite conversation at a social gathering, for example—as well as personal grooming habits. He learned to keep his hair trimmed and combed and his fingernails clean and clipped. In a private journal, he made a list of "maxims," or rules for life. "You can be whatever you resolve to be," he wrote. He also reminded himself to be frugal, industrious, and quiet; to accept just a few close friends; and not to worry about trifles and accidents. Especially, he wanted to be trustworthy. "Sacrifice your life rather than your word," he wrote.

Jackson's honorable character helped to keep down the number of his demerits. Over four years, he did not receive a single demerit for misconduct. Rather, his demerits were all for minor violations of the academy's endlessly strict regulations. When asked whether he ever deliberately disobeyed West Point rules, Jackson could recall only a single incident. One day, he wandered out beyond the academy boundaries without a permit. When he caught sight of an officer nearby, he ducked behind a tree so that he wouldn't get caught. "It was the only one in which I consciously did what I knew to be wrong," he said, as recounted in Robertson's *Stonewall Jackson.*

In his entire four years at West Point, Jackson never spoke to a woman. He preferred to be alone and took long walks up a nearby mountainside to the ruins of Fort Putnam. All that remained of the ancient fort were the rocky skeletons of old buildings. Slabs of stone walls jutted as high as 30 feet in some spots. For some reason, Jackson felt safe and comfortable as he plodded through the ruins. Perhaps the jagged spires of stone reminded him of the white poplars along the banks of the West Fork River back home, where he used to spend afternoons fishing. The view from Fort Putnam was breathtaking. Below, tents dotted the plain outside the academy; the sturdy classroom buildings encircled the drill field like an overprotective parent; and, beyond the campus, the mighty Hudson River rolled toward the Atlantic Ocean. In these quiet moments on the hillside, Jackson could find a bit of peace away from the frantic shuffle of daily drills and classes.

VIEW FROM FORT PUTNAM.
WEST POINT HUDSON RIVER, N.Y.

Shy and quiet, Jackson would often take brief trips up to Fort Putnam, a Revolutionary War fortification that overlooks West Point. There, high above the tents and cabins that shaped his school life, Jackson took a break from the everyday pressures of military training.

Although he was shy and somewhat withdrawn, Jackson managed to form friendships with a wide range of cadets, upper and lower classmen alike. He knew Ulysses S. Grant, William S. Rosecrans, James Longstreet, Ambrose Powell Hill, and, from the class of 1845, Barnard E. Bee. Many of his West Point comrades later became generals and served in the Civil War. At the academy, Jackson had no idea that, one day, he would engage in battles against his classmates and friends.

At the end of his final year, Jackson was a fine young officer of 22. On June 30, 1846, he graduated in the upper third of his class, having compiled one of the most amazing records in the history of West Point. Mired at the bottom with the "immortals" at the outset, at the end he ranked seventeenth out of 59 graduates. He finished fifth in ethics, twelfth in engineering, eleventh in artillery and mineralogy, twenty-first in military tactics. He also finished twenty-fourth out of a total of 213 cadets in conduct, having whittled his demerits down to just seven. His general merit score of 1837.8 was extremely respectable compared with a class high of 2236.5 and a low of 855.7.

During his four years at the academy, Jackson's class rankings had advanced steadily. One fellow cadet was convinced that, if the West Point curriculum had lasted one more year, backwoods Jackson would have graduated at the top of his class. None of this had come easily, however, and years later, Jackson said, "I had to study *very hard* for what I got at West Point." Like the other graduating cadets, Jackson received the rank of brevet second lieutenant. He had to wait until an opening in active duty before he officially became a second lieutenant. That wait proved to be a short one.

In May, the cadets had learned that the United States had declared war on Mexico. Most of the class of 1846 would go straight from graduation to the battlefield. Jackson anxiously hoped to be one of those fortunate cadets to be sent into combat.

On Monday, July 20, Jackson arrived home at Jackson's Mill. He was welcomed by hugs and handshakes from Uncle Cummins and the rest of the Jackson family. According to Robertson's *Stonewall Jackson*, friends in Weston proudly remarked that Jackson "looked every inch a soldier." On his first visit to town, by chance, Jackson ran into Colonel William McKinley, who was holding the annual muster of his 150th Virginia Militia Regiment. At once, McKinley asked Jackson to take command of the lead company.

Somewhat apprehensive, Jackson replied, "I'd like to, Colonel, but I haven't drilled under you. I might not be able to follow your commands."

"What do you mean, son?" McKinley chuckled, as quoted in John Bower's *Stonewall Jackson*. "'Course you can. You're a West Pointer." So, the brevet second lieutenant was introduced to his small company of militiamen at the parade ground. As the march got under way, however, Colonel McKinley became flustered and shouted out the wrong command. Following the command, however strange it seemed, Jackson marched his company off the parade ground. McKinley called after Jackson, but with all the noise and commotion, he did not hear the colonel. His company continued to march up Main Street and through Weston. The colonel, on horseback, galloped

THOMAS JACKSON'S MAXIMS

At West Point, Jackson started keeping a list of "maxims," or rules for life, in a five-by-eight-inch notebook. Some of his entries follow.

- Sacrifice your life rather than your word.
- You can be whatever you resolve to be.
- Through life let your principal object be the discharge of duty.
- Let your conduct toward men have some uniformity.
- Temperance: Eat not to fullness, drink not to elevation.
- Silence: Speak but what may benefit others or yourself; avoid trifling conversation.
- It is not desirable to have a large number of intimate friends.
- Never weary your company by talking too long or too frequently.
- Never try to appear more wise or learned than the rest of the company.

after Jackson. He finally caught up to him in the middle of a meadow. Confused as to why Jackson would take such a ridiculous course, McKinley asked, "Didn't you know enough to stop?"

"Colonel," Jackson said flatly, "I was following orders."

On Wednesday afternoon, just two days after returning home, Jackson received orders to dispatch to Fort Columbus, on Governors Island in New York Harbor. There, he was to report to Captain Francis Taylor, commander of Company K of the First Artillery. Jackson's wish was granted. He was to get his first taste of war. Early on Thursday morning, 22-year-old Thomas Jackson waved good-bye to his family, ready to put his West Point training to the ultimate test. Deep down, he wondered whether he had the courage and bravery it took to be a great military officer.

The Mexican War

Probably no other war waged by the United States had less justice on its side than the Mexican War, which was fought from 1846 to 1848. Ulysses S. Grant—who first gained fame in this war—later described it as "one of the most unjust ever waged by a stronger against a weaker nation." The war pricked many American consciences, but after a year and a half of fighting, President James K. Polk got exactly what he wanted for the Union—New Mexico, California, and what are today the states of Nevada and Utah, plus parts of Colorado and Wyoming. The United States grew nearly one-quarter because of the victory.

The trouble began in 1845, when Texas was annexed to the United States. Texas had won its independence from Mexico in 1836. When Texans wanted to join the Union, Mexico resisted, declaring that this action would start a war. Americans ignored the threat and added Texas as the twenty-eighth and largest state. The chief source of conflict was a disagreement over the border. According to the Mexicans, the northern border of Mexico ran along the Nueces River; the United States claimed that the border was the Rio Grande.

In March 1846, General Zachary Taylor moved 3,500 troops to Camp Texas, in present-day Brownsville. On May 1, Camp Texas was attacked by 6,000 Mexican fighters under General Mariano Arista, but Taylor's army drove them off. The U.S. Army quickly won two other battles—at Palo Alto and Resaca de la Palma. Then, on May 13, the United States officially declared war on Mexico.

Five days later, Taylor invaded Mexico. His advance south was held up for three months, however, as he waited for proper transportation, which the government had promised. However frustrating the delay may have been for General Taylor, it was a stroke of luck for young Thomas Jackson because it allowed him to reach Mexico in time to be part of the war.

Jackson arrived at New York's Fort Columbus in early August of 1846. By the time he got there, however, Captain Francis Taylor had been restationed at Fort Hamilton, on nearby Long Island. Jackson rushed to the new location and found Taylor, but Company K already had left for Monterrey, Mexico. Captain Taylor had stayed behind to round up straggling recruits; he planned to meet up with General Zachary Taylor's forces in Texas and then move on to Monterrey. On August 19, Jackson and 29 other men began a 400-mile overland march to Pittsburgh, Pennsylvania. From there, they made the remainder of the journey by ship. On September 6, the ship *Swatara* reached Newport, Kentucky, across the Ohio River from Cincinnati. Next, the soldiers boarded the *Hendrik Hudson* and moved down the Ohio River toward the mighty Mississippi, which would carry them to New Orleans.

After graduating from the military academy, Jackson earned the rank of second lieutenant and joined U.S. forces in the battle against Mexico. Although the Mexican War was not overwhelmingly popular with the U.S. public, President James K. Polk was able to acquire more land for the United States. Some of the most legendary figures in U.S. history participated in this war, including Ulysses S. Grant, Davy Crockett, Jim Bowie, and Zachary Taylor.

From New Orleans, the men took the *James L. Daly* for the final leg of the trip. The vessel followed the winding Mississippi through thick marshes and into the Gulf of Mexico; the ship hugged the coastline as it pushed southward. Finally, on September 22, the monthlong journey ended, as the *James L. Daly* joined dozens of other ships anchored off Point Isabel, Texas. Earlier, Mexican forces had burned the city, but the harbor remained the base of operations for General Zachary Taylor's force. Jackson was boiling with anticipation; he was eager to experience the thrill of combat. The day that he arrived, however, Mexican forces at Monterrey surrendered to General Taylor, and many people thought that, perhaps, the war was over. In reality, however, none of Taylor's previous victories had made much of an impact on the Mexican army. Although the Mexicans had withdrawn from Monterrey, they still stood firmly defiant. In Monterrey, Taylor acquired a useless town, and he still faced a nation unshaken by their American invaders. Almost 600 miles of hostile country stood between Taylor's army and the enemy's capital, Mexico City. If Thomas Jackson felt any disappointment on hearing news of the surrender, it did not last long.

At last, in mid-October, Captain Taylor's detachment boarded riverboats and started up the Rio Grande. On October 31, they landed at Camargo, a city known for its plaguing mosquitoes, tarantulas, and scorpions. From there, the troops zigzagged through the mountains, trudging up muddy passes in heavy downpours. Finally, on November 24, Jackson's group at last joined the rest of Company K in Monterrey. Jackson spent four days there, performing minimal duties. He bunked in a brick adobe hut with an adjoining orange orchard and a swimming pool.

On November 29, Company K started west with General Taylor's army on a new offensive march. The men advanced 50 miles to the city of Saltillo, which guarded the primary pass that led through the Sierra Madre Mountains and into the rich

valleys beyond. Still hungry for battle, Jackson again was disap-
pointed when, reaching Saltillo on December 2, the army found
it nearly deserted. Captain Francis Taylor's company set up camp
near what became Fort Polk and waited. There were weeks of
inactivity as the men drifted into the new year of 1847.

At about this time, General-in-Chief Winfield Scott entered
the arena. Sixty-year-old Scott had been a general for half his
life, and he looked the part. He stood a burly six-and-a-half-feet
tall. Because he was a stickler for discipline and protocol, the
soldiers jokingly nicknamed him "Old Fuss and Feathers." Scott
reviewed the current military situation—which did not look
promising, with General Taylor's force still 600 miles north of
its target and barely moving at all—and decided to develop a
new strategy. He determined to take command of a new and
larger force and lead it on a joint army and navy operation.

In Scott's vision, his troops would set out by ship, steam
down the Mexican coast, and force their way onto the beaches
at Veracruz, Mexico's main port. From there, American troops
would push inland along the famous National Road. In nine-
teenth century military tactics, true victory meant capturing
the enemy's capital city. The National Road led straight to
Scott's goal: Mexico City. In contrast with Taylor's route, the
National Road offered a 260-mile trek with fewer natural
obstacles than in the desert—obstacles that had been hamper-
ing Taylor's movements.

Scott's plan of attack was not an original one, however.
Three hundred years earlier, Hernan Cortez had followed
the same route in the Spanish conquest of Mexico. This time,
General Scott added a bold element to the plan: He developed
and executed the largest amphibious (combined land and
water) operation in American history to date. To make the plan
work, Scott insisted on building his army with regular army
troops, not volunteers. He needed highly trained soldiers to
carry out the intricate movements effectively. He also wanted
as many West Pointers as possible, even if he had to draw from

Taylor's army to get them. General Scott was convinced that young academy graduates like Jackson possessed better talent, education, and enthusiasm for battle than older army officers.

Jackson's unit departed Saltillo on January 9, 1847, to join Scott along the Mexican coast. The 180-mile sea journey from Veracruz to Lobos Island, where Scott was stationed, took six weeks. During this time, General Scott encountered repeated snags: Transports were not where they were supposed to be, troops were delayed, and supplies ended up in the wrong locations. As March approached, Scott grew hotly impatient. The troops had to get ashore, move across the flat country, and climb into the highlands by the beginning of spring. If they failed to do so, they would face yellow fever, which struck annually with deadly fury. (By the end of the Mexican War, more American soldiers died from disease than by enemy action.)

Finally, on March 4, Jackson and Company K reached the naval anchorage at Lobos Island. Although Scott still had only half the troops and ammunition he had requested, he was eight weeks behind schedule. He decided to move out with what he had—an army of 13,500 men. Company after company climbed from their ships into rowboats and cut through the bobbing waves toward shore. On deck, at sea, Jackson watched as masses of uniformed soldiers lined up in ranks on the shore and marched in step as a band played and American flags rippled against a cloudless sky. It was a sight he would never forget.

FROM VERACRUZ TO THE BATTLE ON BIG HILL

By 10:00 at night, all troops had finally made it ashore. General Scott had expected fierce resistance from the Mexican forces, but nothing happened. The army established a beachhead in front of the 15-foot walls that surrounded Veracruz. Because the beach was too narrow to accommodate the 13,000 American soldiers, many men set up along the sand hills behind the city, and a large number of troops straddled the National Road.

Veracruz was completely isolated. At first, the situation looked grim for Scott's army. The thick city walls seemed too strongly fortified to be scaled, with more than 100 cannons staring down from their gunports with dark, daunting barrels. Then, for several days, violent storms pummeled the coast. When the sky finally cleared, swarms of insects circled the troops.

Scott was anxious to move forward, but not at a needless cost of lives. He decided to force Veracruz's surrender with siege and bombardment. The soldiers spent two weeks digging trenches and securing gun positions. On March 22, the U.S. forces fired their cannons at the seaside fortress. Heavy gunfire from the Mexicans held Scott's men at bay for a time, but the superior American firepower ultimately forced the Mexican fighters to back down. The unsupported garrison of 3,360 Mexican soldiers was no match for Scott's hefty army. During the siege, Jackson bolted from gun to gun like a war veteran as he supervised the salvoes, or simultaneous firings, of the guns. At one point, a cannonball landed within five short steps of him.

On March 27, a white flag of surrender rose above the city wall. Scott's victory at Veracruz came on the heels of Zachary Taylor's inland triumph at Buena Vista on February 23. These two victories put American forces in certain control of the war. The successful conquest thrilled Jackson. His one disappointment was that General Scott allowed the Mexican soldiers to retreat, when they easily could have been taken as prisoners of war. Jackson already was showing signs of his military prowess and his desire for total, unrelenting victory.

Although the five-day bombardment was both loud and spectacular, blasting away gunports and blowing a hole in the city wall, the interior of Veracruz suffered little damage. Inside, the American troops found a charming town of quaint plazas and impressive churches that overlooked a beautiful seafront. On the western side of the city, thick jungle foliage fingered the stone city walls.

THE MEXICANS EVACUATING VERA CRUZ,
and surrendering their Arms to the U.S. Army, under Gen.l Scott.

In planning his attack on the Mexican port of Veracruz, General Winfield Scott insisted on organizing men with military training. Jackson, a graduate of West Point and a second lieutenant, was drafted into Scott's forces and became one of the thousands of soldiers who occupied the beach outside the city stronghold. After initiating a siege against the garrison at Veracruz, Mexican soldiers retreated (*as seen above*) and surrendered the city to U.S. forces.

Spring was well under way. The sun beat down with blistering intensity, and the season's first outbreak of yellow fever alrcady had occurred. In early April, Scott left behind a large garrison to secure Veracruz and started west with the rest of his army, Jackson included, on the National Road.

The march on the overgrown jungle roadway was slow and tedious. Frequently, along the way, bandits and guerrilla fighters attacked the American columns. The road snaked up through a number of mountain passes and towns en route to Mexico City. Mexican general Antonio López de Santa Anna had several ideal spots where he could make a strong stand. No doubt, he would try to keep Scott's forces in the sweltering low country for as long as possible, thereby allowing the dreaded yellow fever to dig its claws into the American army.

General Scott reorganized his army into two divisions, one commanded by William J. Worth and the other by David E. Twiggs. Each division included two brigades of infantry. One of Twiggs's two batteries was Company K of the First Artillery. "Old Davey" Twiggs's division set out for Jalapa, 74 miles from Veracruz and the first sizeable town on the road to Mexico City. At an altitude of 4,000 feet, the city of Jalapa was much healthier than the low-lying costal area. On April 12, only 13 miles from Jalapa, Twiggs's division encountered some of Santa Anna's army. At least 4,000 Mexican soldiers were entrenched atop the hills that rose above both sides of the narrow road, just as it began to climb upward to Jalapa. This pass, as well as the nearby village, was named Cerro Gordo, or Big Hill, after the mammoth, cone-shaped mountain that towered over the region.

Twiggs halted his column of 2,600 troops and waited for Scott to arrive with reinforcements. General Scott reached Big Hill on April 14, increasing the army to 8,500 soldiers. Here, Jackson prepared for his first real battle of the campaign, and of his military career.

Mexican forces swiftly repelled the first two American attacks. Scott decided that any direct attack against the mountain lines would be suicidal. Hoping to find a weak point to strike, he dispatched a group of engineering officers to search for holes in the enemy lines. Then, he formulated a battle plan. Twiggs's division was to move behind Santa Anna's left and rear and secure a position that spanned the National Road. The soldiers would hold there while Scott's troops attacked the Mexicans from the front. As Twiggs's men advanced, however, Mexican soldiers spotted their movement and opened fire. The U.S. Army had no other choice but to return fire and strike the front line. By the time darkness fell, the American forces had successfully pushed the Mexicans toward Cerro Gordo. The fighting stopped for the night.

At 7:00 the next morning, Sunday, April 18, General Scott launched a two-pronged assault on the Mexican army. The enemy line buckled and, before long, collapsed. By mid morning, 1,200 Mexican soldiers were either dead or wounded, and another 3,000 had been taken prisoner. The rest of Santa Anna's forces fled to the capital city. Jackson's company pursued the retreating soldiers for 12 miles, at times coming close enough to send shots from the cannon battery. According to Captain Francis Taylor, as quoted in Robertson's *Stonewall Jackson*, the caissons carrying the ammunition were hauled up early in the night "through the great exertions of Lieutenant Jackson." The troops struggled to pull the artillery wagons up the steep hills of Cerro Gordo.

The battle was a learning experience for Jackson. He studied Scott's tactics: Engineer a strategy to attack the enemy's weak spots and order a swift and hard pursuit to keep the crippled Mexican forces reeling in chaos. The next morning, on the way to Jalapa, Jackson rode over the battlefield. There, he got his first glimpse of a mangled, bloody corpse. He wrote that the sight "filled me with as much sickening dismay as if I had been a woman." Realizing that his sympathy for human suffering could be a weakness, he vowed to toughen up his emotions. To be a great army officer, he needed to overcome this obstacle.

In late April, Jackson was promoted from brevet to regular second lieutenant. The promotion came with a new assignment, to Company G of the First Artillery, under Captain John H. Winder. Instead of handling light battery, Jackson now operated cumbersome heavy artillery. The transfer was not all bad, however. For lack of guns, many heavy artillery companies were used as infantry. To be in command of foot soldiers gave an officer better opportunities to engage in battle and, in battle, opportunities to wage courageous fights. Glory on the battle-field resulted in promotion, which was Jackson's ultimate goal.

Jackson's dreams of combat were quickly shattered. Scott's army was starting toward Perote, 30 miles west—the next stop on the way to Mexico City and American victory. The troops were leaving without Company G, however. Jackson's division had been ordered to stay behind at Jalapa on garrison duty. The war was moving away from Jackson, and although any other officer might have been happy to stay behind, Jackson was mortified. He had come to Mexico to make his mark in the military. For the moment, it seemed as though his chances were over.

GALLANT LIEUTENANT JACKSON

Luckily for Jackson, his days of inactivity and impatience were numbered. On June 18, Company G was ordered to join Scott's army at Puebla, Mexico's second-largest city. Jackson and the rest of his unit started west toward the Sierra Madre Range. A day or so into the journey, Jackson's detachment reached a narrow pass at La Hoya. Suddenly, a band of Mexican guerrillas emerged from the jungle. A hand-to-hand battle quickly ensued. It lasted only a few minutes. With four of their men killed and three captured, the Mexicans turned and disappeared into the jungle.

At Puebla, General Scott designated four artillery companies to become light and mobile units, known more commonly as "flying artillery." One of the units was the First Regiment's Company I, under Captain John B. Magruder. Captain Magruder desperately needed a second lieutenant, but none of the young officers were beating a path to apply for the position. Magruder had a nasty reputation for strict discipline, a fiery temper, and an inflated ego. Jackson was willing to overlook the commander's negative qualities, however, for a chance to be near the enemy. Magruder's reputation as a fighter was well known, and Jackson figured that his company would receive attention wherever it was located. "I knew if there was

GEN. MAGRUDER

Eager to gain military experience and make an impression, Jackson volunteered to be the second lieutenant of General John Magruder's regiment during the Mexican War. A fellow West Point graduate and Southerner, Magruder *(above)* was known for being a difficult leader, but Jackson knew working with the general would expose him to a real battle.

any fighting to be done," Jackson admitted, as recounted in Robertson's *Stonewall Jackson*, "Magruder would be on hand."

Jackson applied at once, but the position was offered to Lieutenant Truman Seymour. This time, Jackson refused to accept defeat. Seymour was one of Jackson's classmates at West Point, and Jackson decided to talk to him. More than once, Seymour had openly expressed his feelings toward Magruder: He had no desire to serve under "Prince John," as the soldiers called him. The two lieutenants petitioned headquarters to reverse their assignments, Jackson's to Company I and Seymour's to Company G. The request was granted, and on July 13, Jackson confidently reported to his new commander.

On August 7, Scott's army resumed its march through the mountains toward Mexico City. More than 10,700 troops moved out in four divisions under generals Worth, Twiggs, Gideon J. Pillow, and John A. Quitman. Somewhere down the road, Santa Anna was waiting, with an army of 30,000 men. Finally, on August 10, Jackson—part of Pillow's division— joined the march. The uphill climb through the mountains was grueling and cold. Once the troops crossed the Continental Divide, however, Jackson viewed the magnificent fertile valley that stretched below the capital city, just 20 miles away.

At this point, the army halted. The geography of the land was tricky and required careful navigating. Between Scott's army and the enemy capital lay three huge lakes surrounded by swamps and a series of causeways that protected the city. Another challenge was the Pedregal, a vast lava field two miles long and five miles wide, laced with ravines. Lacking roadways, the Pedregal was nearly impassable for infantry and impossible for artillery and cavalry. One soldier called it "hell with the fires out."

Again, Scott sent out engineering officers to determine the best route to the town of San Augustin, south of the capital and directly in front of the lava field. Leaving Twiggs's division at Ayotla to trick Santa Anna into thinking that the Americans were planning an attack from the north, Scott moved out with the remaining troops, including Jackson's company. The soldiers spent two days trudging through heavy rains and deep mud. From San Augustin, Mexico City was less than nine miles north. Santa Anna's enormous army was much closer than that, however.

The Mexican commander had secured his position, placing his army squarely between the U.S. Army and Mexico City. He positioned his western flank on top of a hill at Contreras, with infantry and artillery in full force. On the eastern side, the largest force of Mexican fighters set up at Churubusco. In terms of soldiers, Mexico had a three-to-one advantage over the Americans. Santa Anna made one fatal blunder, however. His two key forces—the flanks—were spread too far apart to help each other if needed.

At San Augustin, Scott's army faced the center of the Mexican forces. To march to Mexico City in a straight line, the American forces would have to pass through the towns of San Antonio and Churubusco. Both towns were heavily fortified. To the army's right were swamps and Lake Xochimilco. To the left was the lava field. Through August 16 and 17, Scott's army battled the Mexican cavalry. Meanwhile, the American general was staring at the possibility of engaging in a frontal attack. He wanted to avoid this type of attack at all costs. One reason was that Santa Anna expected it. More importantly, however, in a frontal attack, casualties would be too high. Scott sent Captain Robert E. Lee on one last search for a way through the Pedregal. Lee found a path that was little more than a mule trail. If it could be widened quickly, however, it could serve for artillery. Scott then could use it to circle westward around the Mexican army and attack Santa Anna from the rear.

Early on August 19, 500 of Pillow's infantrymen went to work with pickaxes and shovels to carve a makeshift road through the rocky crevasses of the lava field. At about noon, the work stopped suddenly when shells from the Mexicans' heavy guns began to pound the area. Captain George McClellen rode up to the infantrymen with orders from Pillow: The two American batteries were to move into position at the western edge of the lava field, about 1,000 yards from the enemy. The American artillery returned the Mexicans' fire while the Mexicans scouted the trail and pushed chunks of stone walls into the ravine to block an American advance. Clearly, the two American light artillery units were no match for the Mexican bombardment. Jackson's friend Daniel Harvey Hill, of the 4th Artillery, witnessed the one-sided duel. He later wrote, "Certainly of all the absurd things that Pillow has ever done this was the most silly. Human stupidity can go no farther than this." The only real effect of Pillow's maneuver was to divert attention away from Pillow and Twiggs as the American infantry slowly moved to San Antonio.

Meanwhile, Magruder divided his battery into two sections and positioned them on each side of the howitzers. Jackson manned two cannons on the right, at a turn in the road. The countryside echoed with thundering cannons. Enemy fire pelted the ground around Jackson, but he never once thought of pulling out. He had been ordered to stay there. One by one, his men fell around him. He, too, would have been killed had the course of the battle not changed.

About an hour into the fight, Lieutenant Joseph E. Johnston—in command of Magruder's other section—fell to the ground, shot and dying. Magruder frantically searched for Jackson and the other cannons. Amid the burning smoke and rattling explosions, Magruder feared that Jackson's unit had been overrun and that Jackson, too, was dead. Then, all of a sudden, Jackson emerged from the haze. As Magruder described it in Robertson's *Stonewall Jackson*, "Lieut. Jackson . . . hearing our own fire further in front, advanced in handsome style and . . . kept up the fire with great briskness and effect."

Captain Magruder was thoroughly impressed by young Lieutenant Jackson's coolness and determination under fire. Jackson, too, was awed by the courage he felt in battle. Before this day, he had been unsure of how he would withstand the pressures of the battlefield. Now, he knew that he had the bravery to endure the heat of war.

The battle at Contreras lasted almost three hours before darkness and heavy rains ended the combat. Jackson's company fought valiantly with six-pound cannons and small howitzers against 22 Mexican guns that included several 18-pounders and at least three 8-inch howitzers. During the bombardment, only one American officer was killed and four men wounded. The Americans' guns, however, fared much worse: Out of four, one was destroyed, and two were damaged.

The following day, Scott's men attached Mexican forces at Contreras from the front and the rear. After barely 20 minutes of fighting, the Mexicans broke ranks and fled. General Scott vigorously pursued the enemy and clashed again, briefly, at San Antonio. The remaining fighters of Santa Anna's army retreated to Churubusco. There, the Mexicans reestablished their position, and intense fighting raged through the afternoon. Then, running low on ammunition, Santa Anna abandoned Churubusco. On August 20, 1847, Scott's army suffered 1,000 casualties, including 133 men killed. In contrast, Santa Anna lost about a fourth of his command, with 4,000 dead or wounded and 3,000 captured.

Because Magruder's battery had lost most of their weapons at Contreras, Jackson took no part in the fighting that day. As Scott waged war, Jackson looked over the battlefield from a tall ridge. He became even more convinced of the strategic advantages of flanking maneuvers.

After this devastating Mexican defeat, Scott believed that Santa Anna would want peace, especially as the American army was poised outside the capital. Two weeks passed, but negotiations between the Americans and the Mexicans were at a stalemate. The American troops were 250 miles from their coastal base and supplies, and Mexico City was the only major source of food within reach. General Scott ran out of patience. The last obstacle between the Americans and the capital was Chapultepec, a great castle at the top of a 200-foot hill. Chapultepec was one-quarter of a mile wide and three-quarters of a mile long. Thick stone walls rose on its southern and eastern sides, and the only breaks in the fortress were two small gates. Behind the castle, on the northern side, two causeways led into Mexico City. Scott was unsure how many Mexican troops were inside Chapultepec, but he figured that at least 2,000 soldiers would be needed to defend it. Inside the castle, Mexican general Nicolas Bravo had only 850 troops, 50 of whom were teenage cadets.

At dawn on September 12, the U.S. Army began to bombard the fortress. The steady pounding of cannon fire quickly weakened the small Mexican garrison. General Bravo begged Santa Anna for reinforcements. Because of the intense American firepower, however, Santa Anna could not get the extra soldiers to the castle in time.

The next morning, Scott's army prepared to storm the castle and move on to Mexico City. When the troops reached the causeway behind Chapultepec, they ran headfirst into the enemy. Cannon fire pummeled them from the front, and a large force of Mexican infantry fired muskets at them as quickly as they could load. At the same time, small-arms fire showered down on the Americans from the castle above. The crossfire was thick and accurate, and it kept the Americans at a standstill, unable to advance or retreat. At that point, Jackson rushed forward with his two little six-pound cannons and searched for a good position from which to return fire. The Mexican barrage was dense, however, and musket shot pelted the ground around Jackson like hail.

A few years later, Jackson recalled those chaotic moments: "I was ordered to advance with a section of my battery upon a road swept by the fire of six or eight pieces of Mexican artillery at very short range. It was ticklish work, but there was nothing to be done but to obey orders. So I went on."

The U.S. victories exacted devastating casualties for Mexico, but their leader, General Santa Anna, refused to admit defeat and General Winfield Scott ordered his troops to march on to Chapultepec, a Mexican fort. Jackson, exhilarated from winning at the Battle of Contreras, joined Scott's forces with two six-pounder cannon and later described the dangerous experience as "ticklish work."

As soon as Jackson reached the main road, the Mexicans opened fire, killing or maiming all twelve of the horses that had pulled Jackson's two cannons. Jackson found himself standing among the corpses of six horses that still were harnessed to the artillery wagon. At that moment, Lieutenant George H. Gordon, a West Point classmate of Jackson's, galloped with a unit of cavalry to where Jackson stood. With a salute, Gordon shouted, "Well, Old Jack, it seems to me you are in a bad way!" Through the clanging din of cavalry swords and the pounding of hooves, Jackson called back, "'Pears I am!"

Jackson's unit was in disarray. One cannon was so damaged that, at first, it could not be moved. Terrified gunners ducked behind boulders and bushes to find cover. Everyone except

Jackson teetered on the edge of panic. Jackson darted back and forth on the road as bullets whizzed past, ricocheting off rocks and kicking up puffs of dust. "There's no danger!" he shouted to his scattering men, in an attempt to build their confidence. It was no use, however. The never-ending volley of bullets told them otherwise.

At one point, a cannonball zipped between Jackson's legs. He never shuddered. Several privates stepped up to help the brave young officer, and Jackson sent one of them to get more men. General Worth rode past the area just in time to see Jackson standing alone against a great part of the Mexican army. Worth told him to leave the field, but Jackson insisted that it would be more dangerous to fall back than to push forward. Jackson then took aim with his cannon and continued to fire. Next, Captain Magruder galloped toward Jackson's position. As he approached, his horse toppled to the ground, felled by a fatal bullet. Magruder picked himself up and ran to Jackson's side. With Magruder's help, Jackson got both of his cannons into working positions and began sighting and firing at the enemy.

For Jackson, it was a scene of which legends are made: a tall, young soldier, out in front of an entire American army, fearlessly facing overwhelming odds as he replied with small volleys to massive enemy firepower.

General Worth rushed in a brigade just as the Mexican defenses at Chapultepec gave way. At last, the castle fell. The Mexicans fought on, however. Santa Anna desperately tried to rally his troops at the gates of Mexico City. General Scott ordered his troops to push forward before the Mexican forces could reorganize.

Meanwhile, Jackson had attached his cannons to wagons and had pulled them to the San Cosme Gate, at the entrance to the capital. In the rush, his unit had got ahead of the main army. He met up with two officers and about 40 men who were pursuing the Mexican army down the Tacubaya Causeway.

Jackson rumbled up with his cannon and offered them the use of his artillery if they wished to keep going. Just then, Magruder arrived on the scene. He ordered Jackson and the other officers to fall back and wait for the rest of the army. Jackson and the others begged him to let them continue, however, and Magruder gave in.

Almost at once, the small unit came face-to-face with 1,500 Mexican lancers, who barreled down on the Americans. On open ground, these cavalrymen would have overrun the Americans, but because they were galloping on the causeway, they had to ride in tight formation. Thinking quickly, Jackson opened fire on the charging horsemen. Each cannon blast cut lanes, or openings, through them.

The fight for Mexico City ended at nightfall on September 13. The city's walls had been breached. The Mexicans had not yet been defeated, however. By nightfall, the Americans had lost 130 men, with 720 more wounded. Mexican losses were more than 3,000 and included the capture of 820 soldiers and 6 generals.

That night, Jackson camped on a hill that overlooked the San Cosme Gate. He replayed the afternoon's events in his mind. It had been the most spectacular day of his life. He was a hero. He had met crisis with courage and valor. Furthermore, such behavior seemed to be instinctive for him. He knew that, even during intense combat, he would remain composed and in control. It was almost as if the confusion triggered a calmness that allowed him to make quick, rational decisions.

The next morning, Jackson expected to enter Mexico City with the first American troops. Instead, he was ordered to cover the western gate with his cannons. Throughout the day, Scott's army advanced into the capital to deliver the final blows to the Mexican forces. Scott's brilliant campaign had ended in victory.

On February 2, 1848, the Treaty of Guadalupe Hidalgo was signed, officially ending the Mexican War. Everyone still was talking about Lieutenant Thomas Jackson's bravery on the battlefield. General Pillow and Captain Magruder wrote glowing reports about the young officer. General Worth gave Jackson lavish praise, even though Jackson was not under his command. Worth wrote, "After advancing some four hundred yards we came to a battery which had been assailed by a portion of Magruder's field guns—particularly the section under the gallant Lieut. Jackson, who, although he had lost most of his horses and many of his men, continued chivalrously at his post combating with noble courage." Soon after, Jackson was promoted to brevet major.

In just six months in the field, Jackson had advanced from brevet second lieutenant, to first lieutenant, to brevet major. By the beginning of July 1848, he was on a ship headed back to New Orleans. Almost two years earlier, he had left for Mexico as an anxious, green young officer. Now, with a beard and mustache, he returned not only as a grown man, but also as a war hero.

The
Lexington Years

After the Mexican War, Jackson took a brief leave to visit his sister Laura and other relatives in Virginia. He then was ordered to report back to Fort Hamilton, on New York's Long Island. As he bid farewell to his family, he had no way of knowing that he would never see his Uncle Cummins again. In 1848, gold was discovered in California. Like thousands of other Americans, Cummins caught "gold fever." He headed west, hoping to find his fortune. Sadly, Cummins Jackson never got his chance. Shortly after he reached California, he was struck with typhoid fever. He died on December 4, 1849. The news of his uncle's death came as a terrible blow to Jackson; Cummins was the only father he had ever known.

At Fort Hamilton, Jackson performed routine garrison duty. He served as commander of Company K and as company

Shortly after their mother remarried, Jackson and his sister Laura *(above)* were sent to Jackson's Mill to live with relatives. As his closest relative, Jackson frequently corresponded with Laura and visited her in Virginia after he completed his service in the Mexican War.

quartermaster and commissary. He frequently was called to court-martial duty as well. Jackson seemed to enjoy his duties, and he quickly picked up on the business side of military operations. As an eligible young bachelor, he also began to socialize with the local ladies. Just outside the walls of the fort, a community known as the Narrows bustled with activity. Many New

Yorkers visited this section of New Utrecht, in what is now Brooklyn, as a summer escape from the city.

During this time, Jackson became engrossed in two subjects that influenced him for the rest of his life: health and religion. His trip back to New York from Virginia had been a rough one. The conditions, which included bitter winter winds and rutted mountain roads, had brought on an attack of rheumatism, a condition that causes pain in the muscles and joints. His weakened strength greatly limited his activities. At the same time, his eyes became extremely sensitive to light. In a letter to Laura, he complained that he could not gaze out a window for long and that opening his eyes out of doors was excruciating. Even the flame of a candle was unbearable to look at.

Jackson also suffered from the digestive disorder dyspepsia, which he called "my disease." To calm his sour stomach, he switched to a plain diet of lightly salted meat, water and tea, egg yolks, and some vegetables. He avoided foods that were difficult to digest, such as cabbage, lettuce, fruits, and nuts. Because so many foods caused his stomach to become upset, he carried his own foods with him to banquets and balls. He also engaged in rigorous exercise and went to bed early every night. When he attended social functions, he left when tattoo sounded.

Jackson became a devout Christian. On April 29, 1849, the 25-year-old officer was baptized at St. John's Episcopal Church, just outside the fort. Serious and pious, he let nothing interfere with his worship. As quoted in Byron Farwell's *Stonewall: A Biography of General Thomas J. Jackson*, he told his sister that he wanted "to live more nearly to God."

In December 1850, Jackson's routine garrison duty at Fort Hamilton came to an end. He was transferred to Company E, which was stationed at Fort Meade, in central Florida. The fort was 23 miles south of present-day Lakeland and about 40 miles east of Tampa. At that time, Tampa was a village of 200 people that was recovering from a recent hurricane. Compared with Fort Hamilton, this outpost near the Everglades, surrounded by sand and palmetto trees, was a crude wilderness barracks. It certainly lacked the personal and social niceties of Long Island.

At Fort Meade, Jackson's commanding officer was 33-year-old Captain and Brevet Major William Henry French, a tall, robust fellow who had graduated from West Point nine years before Jackson. In Florida, French had fought against the Creek and the Seminole in the bloody Seminole War of 1834–1842. Like Jackson, he had won two brevets in the Mexican War. Captain French was witty and intelligent and had a reputation of being an excellent light artilleryman. He also was happily married.

Although Jackson enjoyed leading scout parties through the Everglades, he had a hard time getting along with French. The two officers argued about who was in charge of construction work at the fort. After Jackson was rejected for a commanding position, he set out to prove that French was unworthy of his post. By twisting some flimsy rumors, Jackson accused French of having an affair with a servant girl. In retaliation, French filed charges against Jackson. The complaints finally made their way to General Scott, who dismissed the matter with a stern rebuke to both officers. By this time, however, Jackson already had accepted an offer to teach natural and experimental science at the Virginia Military Institute (VMI) in Lexington, Virginia. He resigned from the army and became a professor.

Before starting his new teaching position, Jackson spent some time in New York. There, he was invited to a dinner party given by Dr. Roland and Marie Houghton, a prominent couple who believed in the potential wonders of hydropathy to cure illnesses. This therapy uses water to treat disease, both through drinking and through external applications, such as hot baths. Jackson refused to eat even the plainest foods at the Houghtons' party. This caught the sympathetic eye of Mrs. Houghton, who had written the book *Water Cure for Ladies* in 1844. It also grabbed the attention of her father, Dr. Lowry Barney, a well-known physician who investigated strange sicknesses. Dr.

Barney firmly believed that proper diet and exercise could cure any illness. That evening, Barney asked Jackson about his health troubles, and Jackson explained his symptoms in great detail. Barney invited Jackson to spend some time at his farm in the far northwest corner of New York, near Lake Ontario. Jackson accepted the invitation and spent six weeks in the quiet countryside, feasting on a diet of buttermilk and cornbread and beginning a water-therapy treatment. Every day, he took a brisk two-mile walk. By the time he left, his health had greatly improved.

As a departing Jackson carried his bags to the door, Dr. Barney rattled off instructions. Jackson was to continue his diet and exercise routine. In addition, Barney said, he was to overcome stress, which aggravated his stomach problems. The doctor suggested that not only relaxation and recreation but also marriage would help him reduce stress. Thrilled with the results of his treatment, Jackson dutifully obeyed the doctor's orders, except the marriage part, at least for the time being. Eager to start his new career at VMI, Jackson left for Lexington in the early summer of 1851. The trip to Lexington from upstate New York took about a week.

Before VMI became a school, the facility served as an arsenal. Overlooking the North Branch of the James River (now the Maury River) on the northern edge of Lexington, the arsenal once housed 30,000 muskets left over from the War of 1812. When the school first opened, in 1839, there were 33 cadets. By the time Jackson arrived, in 1851, enrollment had grown to 117 young men.

At the end of the summer, when classes were ready to resume, construction of a new barracks had not yet been completed. To keep the cadets occupied and out of the way of the construction, Major Jackson took them on a marching tour of the countryside. They marched to the popular Virginia springs, or spas, such as Rockbridge Alum, Bath Alum, and Warm Springs. These springs were not only popular as health

After the Mexican War, Jackson spent time in Florida and New York before taking a teaching position at the Virginia Military Institute *(above)*. In addition to teaching physics, Jackson also gave lessons on artillery tactics and drilled the cadets. Highly respected at the school, though not for teaching, Jackson would be called upon to lead the cadets into tense situations later in his career.

spas, but also drew many tourists. At each spring, the cadets attracted quite an audience. Their daily parades and guard mountings became a popular attraction. As soon as Jackson received word that the barracks were finished, he marched the cadets back to the institute. In less than a month, the cadets had marched nearly 100 miles.

An architectural and engineering marvel, the new quarters boasted gaslights and central heating. Fortunately, Jackson got the opportunity to enjoy these luxuries. He shared a room on the third floor—or stoop, as floors were called at VMI and West Point—of the east tower with Major William Gilham. The following year, Jackson moved to the fourth stoop, where he roomed with a young graduate instructor, Lieutenant

Thomas A. Harris, who later became a surgeon in the Confederate Army.

Classes began in late September. Jackson taught two one-and-a-half-hour classes in the morning and artillery drill in the afternoon. The routine at VMI was much like the one Jackson had experienced at West Point. At dawn, reveille was sounded by fife and drum. Cadets ate breakfast at 7:00 and reported for guard mount at 8:00. Then, they scurried off to morning classes from 8:30 to 1:00. After lunch, afternoon classes ran from 2:00 to 3:30, followed by a drill period and dress parade before supper.

During drill, Jackson at first taught from a book by Winfield Scott titled *Infantry Tactics*. In 1855, however, this text was replaced by *Rifle and Light Infantry Tactics*, a two-volume work by Colonel William Joseph Hardee, who had been commandant of cadets at West Point. Jackson supplemented the drills with recitations from several artillery books. For artillery drill, Jackson used four brass 6-pounders and two 12-pound howitzers that had been designed and built specifically for the institute by Watervliet Arsenal in New York. Each big gun was about 200 pounds lighter than its real-life counterpart. The 6-pounders weighed 564 pounds and the howitzers weighed 578 pounds. This six-gun battery was splendid, but Jackson had no horses to use for artillery instruction. He organized cadets to act as horses to pull the guns, caissons, and limbers. After harnessing the cadets, he yelled, "Limbers and caissons . . . trot, march!" One day, a cadet refused to trot at Jackson's order. The cadet was required to write a formal excuse explaining his behavior. In the paper, as quoted in Farwell's *Stonewall*, he gave a witty explanation. "I am a natural pacer," he wrote, referring to the type of horse used to set the pace in races.

Artillery drills came easy for Jackson. Classroom teaching of such subjects as optics, acoustics, astronomy, and analytical mechanics was another story, however. Jackson lectured dryly, straight from his textbook, without adding any additional illustrations to clarify the coursework. If a cadet asked him to explain a point, Jackson merely reread the passage from the book. He never rephrased the material, or tried to word it in a different way. Because he was clumsy with his hands, his classroom experiments usually failed. His incompetence was visible to both students and faculty. In a letter home, one cadet wrote that his optics class was very difficult, mostly because it was "taught by such a *hell of a fool*, whose name was Jackson." Even the superintendent had to admit that Jackson "was no *teacher*, and he lacked the tact required in getting along with his classes. Every officer and every cadet respected him for his many sterling qualities. He was a brave man, a conscientious man, a good man, but he was not a professor." In Jackson's mind, however, he was a successful teacher. He insisted that if God sent him a task, he also would grant him the power and knowledge to perform it.

For some reason, perhaps because he had poor hearing, Jackson was unable to maintain order in the classroom. The free-spirited and rowdy young men of Virginia had a tendency to be disruptive and disrespectful. At times, Jackson seemed undisturbed by their "paper pellets," catcalls, and dog barks. When cadets were blatantly disrespectful, however, he was quick to court martial them. During his 10 years at VMI, Jackson served on many courts-martial, and he often was the accuser. One such case involved Cadet James A. Walker, a top student and a senior who was scheduled to graduate in less than two months. The incident started when Walker chose to argue with Jackson. When Jackson ordered him to be quiet, Walker refused to back down. To make matters worse, Walker's written excuse to Jackson was both insolent and unremorseful. Walker was expelled from the institute for his actions. Fuming, he threatened to kill Jackson. Even though the young hothead was armed and roaming the streets, Jackson refused to alter his daily routine. He walked his usual route to and from classes and remained unshaken until the cadet's father finally showed up to take the boy back home.

ELLIE AND ANNA

"Of all the places which have come under my observation in the United States, this little village [of Lexington] is the most beautiful," Jackson wrote in a letter to Laura in 1852, at the end of his first year at VMI. In 1850, Lexington had a population of 1,743, including 638 African Americans. Almost immediately, Jackson felt at home. One thing was missing, however: a wife.

In February 1852, Jackson became friends with Elinor (Ellie) Junkin, a daughter of the Reverend Dr. George Junkin, president of Washington College in Lexington. Jackson had met Ellie shortly after he moved to town; the two formed a close friendship when they began teaching Sunday school together at Lexington Presbyterian Church. At this time, there were three Junkin daughters living at home: 33-year-old Margaret, whom everyone called Maggie; 28-year-old Ellie; and Julia, who was 18 years old. Maggie and Ellie were practically inseparable. The two sisters shared a room, dressed alike, and spent most of the day together. Of the two, Maggie, a poet and writer, was more intellectual. Ellie, born less than a year after Jackson, was prettier, more cheerful, and less studious than her older sister.

Isabella Hill, the wife of Jackson's friend, West Point graduate Daniel Harvey Hill, played matchmaker for the couple. One day, as he talked to Daniel Hill, Jackson admitted that he had been having some confusing feelings. "I don't know what has changed me," he told Hill, as recounted in Robertson's *Stonewall Jackson*. "I used to think [Ellie] plain, but her face now seems to me all sweetness." Hill chuckled and gave Jackson a pat on the back. "You are in love!" he said. "That's what's the matter!"

Before long, Ellie Junkin and Thomas Jackson began to see each other often. The courtship was a bumpy one; however, it probably was plagued by Ellie's possessive older sister. Perhaps

While living in Lexington, Virginia, Jackson found himself admiring Ellie Junkin, daughter of a local minister. Though Ellie's sister did not approve of him, Jackson was deeply in love and was distraught when it appeared Ellie had ended the relationship. The couple, however, prevailed and was later married.

worried that she was about to lose her closest friend to marriage, Maggie persuaded Ellie to break off the relationship with Jackson. Late that same night, utterly distraught, Jackson pounded at the door of Daniel and Isabella Hill. He pleaded with Isabella to go to talk with Ellie the next day. Isabella tried to talk Ellie into giving Jackson another chance, but the young lady's mind seemed to be made up.

The breakup threw Jackson into anguish. Some of his friends worried that he was losing his mind. On one occasion, he talked wildly to Hill about becoming a missionary and dying in a foreign land. Eventually, however, Ellie changed her mind. She chose Jackson over her sister, and the couple became engaged. As was the custom at the time, Ellie wanted to keep the engagement secret, except to immediate family. To honor her request, Jackson even kept Laura completely in the dark. His dear sister did not find out about Ellie until after the wedding. Because of this secrecy, Laura held a stiff grudge against her brother for quite some time.

At sunset on Thursday, August 4, 1853, Thomas and Ellie were married by Dr. Junkin in the family parlor. Shortly afterward, the couple left for their honeymoon. Perhaps in an effort to comfort Maggie, they brought her along on the trip, even though Jackson probably was less than thrilled to have his sister-in-law along on his wedding trip. They traveled first to Philadelphia, then to West Point, and finally to Niagara Falls. At Niagara Falls, the group ventured out in a small boat to the foot of the falls. Maggie, terror stricken, wrestled to get out of her seat. Pinning her down with a strong grip, Jackson asked one of the rowers, "How often have you crossed here?"

"I have been rowing people across, sir, for twelve years," the man replied.

"Did you ever meet with an accident?" Jackson inquired.

"Never, sir," said the boatman.

"Never were capsized, never lost a life?" repeated Jackson.

"Nothing of the kind, sir," the man confirmed.

Turning to Maggie, Jackson said in a firm voice, "You hear what the boatman says, and unless you think you can take oars and row better than he does, sit still and trust him as I do." From Niagara Falls, the party traveled down the St. Lawrence River to Montreal and Quebec and then headed back through Boston and New York.

The following summer, Jackson got word that his sister Laura had lost a child. He decided that he and Ellie needed to visit her in Beverly, West Virginia. Ellie was six months pregnant at the time, and the rough and jolting ride through the mountains would be difficult for her. Jackson insisted on making the trip, although the stagecoach ride was, indeed, torturous. The visit with Laura offered healing. At once, Ellie and Laura became friends. Any lingering anger about the secret wedding vanished.

The long and tiring journey took a heavier toll on fragile Ellie than she at first realized, however. Three months after the visit, on October 22, Ellie gave birth to a stillborn baby boy. Despite this tragedy, Ellie at first seemed to have survived without any ill effects. The doctor left, and Jackson sat down on the bed to comfort his grieving wife. Almost immediately, Ellie began to feel excruciating pain in her abdomen. Jackson called the doctor back. Apparently, Ellie had uncontrollable internal bleeding. Within several hours, she was gone.

Jackson was devastated by the deaths of his wife and son. His agony was so deep that friends again worried he was losing his mind. On October 24, Ellie and her newborn baby were buried in a single coffin in the Junkin family plot. Although he did not weep at the funeral, the pain Jackson suffered was apparent in his eyes. Unable to cope on his own, he turned to his faith for strength. "The Lord giveth and the Lord taketh away, blessed be the name of the Lord," he wrote in a letter to his sister, as quoted in Robertson's *Stonewall Jackson*. "It is His will that my dearest wife and child should not longer abide with me, and as it is His holy will, I am perfectly reconciled to the sad bereavement, though I deeply mourn my loss." In another letter, several weeks later, he said, "I look forward to the day when I shall join *her* . . . [I] have joy in hope of a future reunion when the wicked cease from trembling and the weary are at rest."

In the months that followed Ellie's death, Jackson and Maggie Junkin became faithful friends. She was, perhaps, the one person who could comfort him because she felt the same grief that he did. Sorrow over dear, departed Ellie was their common bond. It brought them close together, like brother and sister.

Ellie's death moved Jackson to take a trip back to his roots, to seek out the graves of his family. In the summer of 1855, he returned to Jackson's Mill. So much had changed since he last had been there that it hardly looked like the town he knew. In Clarksburg, he visited the graves of his father and his older sister, Elizabeth. Finding that there were no headstones, he made arrangements to have the site cleaned up and grave markers put in place. Next, in search of his mother's grave, he traveled by steamboat down the Ohio River to Point Pleasant, up the sparsely settled Kanawha Valley to Hawks Nest, and, finally, to the hamlet of Ansted. There, a man claimed to know the spot where Julia Jackson had been buried and offered to show it to Jackson. When they got to the site, however, there was no marker on the ground and no way of knowing for sure whether it truly was Julia Jackson's grave. Disheartened, Jackson left for Lexington without finding his mother's resting place.

The following summer, Jackson decided to fulfill his lifelong dream of a European vacation. On July 9, 1856, he boarded the Cunard steamship *Asia*. On Monday July 21, the ship docked at Liverpool, England. From there, Jackson took a train to the city of Chester and checked into a hotel. From Chester he traveled north to tour Scotland and then traveled through England—from York, to Ely, to Cambridge, and, at last, to London. He then sailed to Antwerp, in Belgium, to kick off a classic tour of the continent.

Near Brussels, also in Belgium, Jackson visited the Waterloo battlefield. Strangely, it was the only battlefield he toured in Europe. Looking over the field, he decided that Napoleon Bonaparte should have launched his main attack on the village of Mont Saint-Jean instead of the Château of Hougoumont. Jackson next traveled up the valley of the Rhine River through Germany. He stopped in Cologne, Bonn, Frankfurt am Main, Heidelberg, Baden-Baden, and Strasbourg, where he marveled at the astronomical clock. He then crossed into Switzerland, where he visited Basle, Thun, Bern, Freiburg, and Geneva. He traveled through the Alps on Napoleon's route through the Simplon Pass. In Italy, he saw Lake Como and Lake Maggiore and toured Milan, Venice, Mantua, Verona, Modena, Florence (one of his favorite cities), Pisa, Leghorn (Livorno), and Naples. He completed this whirlwind tour in an impressive six weeks.

Jackson returned to Lexington revitalized and ready to tackle a new academic year. When he finally started to think about love again, his thoughts drifted back to the summer of 1853. In that year, Isabella Hill's younger sister, Mary Anna, had come to town for a long stay. During her visit, Jackson had played older brother to her and spent much time entertaining the young North Carolina belle. Anna—never called Mary—was the fourth child of the Reverend Dr. Robert Hall Morrison, a Presbyterian minister and the first president of David College, a Presbyterian college for men that was founded in 1836. After his return from Europe, Jackson wrote Anna a letter in which he recalled the "blissful memories" of that summer when they first met. Before long, the couple began to exchange letters. During Jackson's second visit to see Anna in North Carolina, he proposed to her.

On July 16, 1857, a blistering hot afternoon, the couple was married at the Morrisons' Cottage Home, about 20 miles northeast of Charlotte, North Carolina. Once again, Jackson

After the devastating death of his wife and son, Jackson visited his childhood home at Jackson's Mill and then traveled through Europe. Upon his return to Lexington, he met Anna, the sister of a close neighborhood friend, and eventually fell in love with her. They were later married in North Carolina.

took his new bride on a honeymoon to Niagara Falls. When they arrived back in Lexington, the newlyweds boarded at the Lexington Hotel until they could afford a home of their own. In January 1858, they moved into a two-story brick-and-stone house on Washington Street in downtown Lexington. Before they were completely settled, however, tragedy struck. On April 30, Anna gave birth to a girl, whom the couple named Mary Graham, after Anna's mother. Over the next couple of weeks, the baby fell deathly ill. Her skin turned a yellowish hue; at times, she was almost comatose. On May 25, little Mary died of jaundice, a liver problem that causes too much bile pigment, or bilirubin, to build up in the blood. A few weeks later, Anna suffered another blow. Her adored sister Eugenia died of a stroke. Also in July, one of Jackson's close friends died of a lingering illness.

This string of deaths and devastation caused Jackson to succumb to a series of illnesses. He suffered a swollen throat and ear passage. The inflammation became so serious that he was almost entirely deaf in his right ear. Then, in August, he had to have his right tonsil removed. For the rest of his life, Jackson battled bouts of sickness, both minor and severe.

Shortly after the death of Anna's sister Eugenia, Eugenia's three-year-old son came to live with the Jacksons. The boy stayed with them until war broke up the household. In late October, Laura's 13-year-old son, Thomas Jackson Arnold, also came to live with the Jacksons in Lexington. The boy stayed with them until the following July. Desperately wanting to be a father, Jackson enjoyed spending time with Thomas. He helped him with his lessons and took him on long walks. They also worked together in Jackson's prized vegetable garden.

The Jacksons owned six slaves. Before he married Anna, Jackson had bought two slaves, Albert and Amy. According to Anna Jackson, Albert had asked Jackson to purchase him; he offered to buy his freedom by working as a hotel waiter. Amy, who was about to be sold as payment for a debt, also asked Jackson to purchase her. A fine cook and housekeeper, Amy wanted to work for a "good Christian family." Hetty, the Jacksons' chambermaid, had been Anna's nurse; Dr. Morrison transferred her ownership to Anna when the Jacksons moved to Virginia. Not wanting to separate Hetty from her two sons, Cyrus, age 12, and George, 16, Dr. Morrison let them go with the Jacksons as well. The sixth Jackson slave was Emma, a four-year-old orphan whom Jackson had taken in on the urging of an elderly lady in Lexington. Jackson thought that Anna might enjoy training the child and teaching her to read. Anna found Emma to be troublesome, however, and never took to her the way Jackson had hoped.

Strict but kind, Jackson treated his slaves well. He called them for daily family worship, brought them to church on Sunday, and gave them Sunday-school lessons. Years after the Civil War, Anna asserted that Jackson would have preferred to see the slaves be free. He believed, however, that the Bible taught that slavery had been established by God. He therefore accepted slavery as a righteous institution.

In addition to being a respected VMI professor, Jackson became something of a businessman. In 1859, he bought a small, 18-acre farm on the edge of town. With the help of his slaves, he began to grow crops of wheat, corn, and other vegetables and planted an orchard. In April 1860, he and several partners purchased a tannery and a lot, 100 feet by 131 feet, on Randolph Street in Lexington. He later bought 320 acres in the Blue Ridge, about eight miles from Lexington. At last, life started to offer Jackson some prosperity and happiness. His comfortable home life was about to come to an abrupt end, however, in ways that he could never have imagined.

War

John Brown was a nervous, high-strung, wildly religious man. He believed that God had given him a mission to abolish slavery, even by violent means. In 1856, he had led a seven-man gang that brutally murdered five Kansas settlers by splitting their heads with broadswords in an incident that came to be known as the Pottawatomie Massacre. After a brief but bloody battle with the proslavery men of the area, Brown and his abolitionist partners fled from the territory to Canada. There, he hatched a plot to liberate African-American slaves and, with them, found a new nation in the mountains of western Virginia, in which he would be the commander-in-chief. The first step in his scheme was to attack the U.S. arsenal at Harpers Ferry, Virginia, in what is now West Virginia. He planned to distribute the arms captured there to local slaves, thus instigating a rebellion.

On the night of October 16, 1859, Brown and a posse of 21 men, including four of his sons, launched an assault on the arsenal at Harpers Ferry. Because the arsenal was defended by only one guard, this capture was not a difficult feat. During the siege, one man in Brown's group was killed: an unarmed, free African-American railroad worker. Next, Brown took 60 prominent citizens hostage. One of the hostages was a descendant of George Washington. Brown then cut telegraph wires and blocked railroad tracks in an attempt to keep military reinforcements away from Harpers Ferry. Originally, he had hoped to rally 500 slaves to join his "army," but only 10 enslaved men mustered up enough courage to flee their owners and join Brown's rebellion.

Within hours of the attack, local militia and every townsman with a weapon showed up at Harpers Ferry. During the fight that followed, Brown and his handful of men were forced to take refuge in a small brick firehouse. Two more of his band were killed and used as target practice by the enraged townsmen. Word of Brown's raid was sent to Washington, D.C., by telegraph. The next day, a small force of Marines, led by U.S. Army lieutenant Robert E. Lee, was hastily dispatched to Harpers Ferry. When Brown refused to surrender, the Marines launched a swift assault. Within three minutes, all of Brown's men were either killed or captured. Of the raiders, 10 men were killed outright or mortally wounded, including two of Brown's sons. Seven men were taken prisoner, including John Brown. Five raiders managed to escape. During the fight, Brown's men killed five Marines and wounded nine others.

Although Brown argued that he should be treated as a prisoner of war rather than a criminal, federal authorities handed him over to the Virginia courts. Justice was swift. The trial

One of the troubling events leading up to the Civil War included the raid on Harpers Ferry, the location of a large armory. Led by John Brown (*in beard*), an ardent abolitionist, a group of men seized the cache of weapons, intending to distribute them to slaves in hopes of inciting a rebellion, and then held a number of people hostage. This attempt failed and Jackson was on hand to witness Brown's execution.

began on October 27; four days later, the jury convicted Brown of treason, conspiring with slaves to commit treason, and murder. He was sentenced to be hanged on December 2.

Brown's raid at Harpers Ferry electrified both the North and the South. With sensational drama, the incident brought the institution of slavery—along with all of its accompanying social, economic, and political issues—into bold view. Tensions between Northern and Southern states had been stretched steadily tighter throughout the 1850s. With each passing year, an American civil war seemed more and more certain. Numerous events—some, such as Eli Whitney's invention of the cotton gin, dating back as far as 1793—pushed Northerners and Southerners farther apart. The combination of Eli Whitney's invention and slave labor had made cotton "king" in the South. Whitney's machine separated cotton fibers from the hulls and seeds and drastically reduced the time it took to complete that formerly tedious process. The cotton gin allowed plantation owners to make big profits growing large crops of cotton. Those plantation owners relied on African and, later, African-American slaves to work in their vast fields.

Throughout the South, in fact, the economy was based on agriculture. In addition to cotton, plantation owners grew and exported such crops as tobacco, indigo, and rice. Because slaves performed the fieldwork, the Southern economy depended on slavery to prosper. In the North, the economy did not depend on slave labor. Instead, it was based on industry and small businesses. Many Northerners believed that slavery was morally wrong and should be outlawed. By the 1850s, most Northern states had made slavery illegal, even though free blacks in the North did not have the same rights and opportunities as Northern whites.

As America expanded into lands gained in the Louisiana Purchase and the Mexican War, the question arose as to whether the new territories should allow slavery or be free. The slaveholding Southern states had a much smaller white population than the Northern free states. Under the Constitution, the number of congressmen to be elected to the House of Representatives from each state was based on the total white population of that state. By 1820, rapid growth in the North had left the Southern states with less than 45 percent of the seats in the House. The Senate, on the other hand, had the same number of representative, from each state and was balanced between 11 Northern states and 11 Southern states.

In 1818, the Missouri Territory applied for statehood. Missouri wanted to be a slave state—a state in which slavery would be legal. To admit Missouri as a slave state would give Southern slave states a majority of seats in the Senate. New York representative James Tallmadge introduced an amendment that prohibited any further growth of slavery in Missouri. Furthermore, the amendment said, any slave born in Missouri would be emancipated, or freed, at age 25. The statehood bill easily passed the House, but when the Senate did not vote for it, the bill died.

Then, in 1819, the free territory of Maine also applied for statehood. Speaker of the House Henry Clay saw an opportunity to keep a balance of free and slave states in the Senate. He proposed that Maine and Missouri be admitted to the Union together, one as a free state and one as a slave state. Clay persuaded Northern congressmen to drop the amendment forbidding slavery in Missouri. At the same time, the new bill would limit slavery to territory below the 36°30' north latitude, a line that marked the southern border of Missouri. This agreement left the unsettled portion of the Louisiana Purchase—lands north and west of Missouri—free from slavery. The only area in which slavery could spread was into present-day Arkansas and Oklahoma. The proposal, known as the Missouri Compromise, was passed, and conflict was postponed for a time.

Thirty years later, Congress passed the Compromise of 1850. This act of legislation was created to keep Southern states from seceding from, or leaving, the Union to form their own separate government. Proposed again by Clay, the compromise admitted California as a free state and allowed the rest of the land acquired in the Mexican War—land that today is Utah and New Mexico—to be admitted as slave states. At the same time, Congress passed a Fugitive Slave Act. At times, slaves escaped from the South and fled to free Northern states. These runaway, or fugitive, slaves often used the Underground Railroad—a system of safe houses through which abolitionists helped runaway slaves escape to freedom.

Slaveholders wanted to make sure that anyone who helped a runaway slave was punished. The Fugitive Slave Act of 1850 stated that all escaped slaves must be returned to their owners. If any person failed to turn in an escaped slave, he or she could be slapped with a hefty fine, imprisoned, or both. Many Northerners chose to ignore this law. In fact, many Northern states passed their own laws concerning runaway slaves that made the Fugitive Slave Act basically null and void. The refusal of Northern states to enforce the Fugitive Slave Act was one of the reasons that South Carolina finally seceded from the Union in 1860.

In 1854, Congress passed the Kansas-Nebraska Act, which overruled the Missouri Compromise. Instead of requiring states above 36°30' north latitude to be admitted as free states, the Kansas-Nebraska Act allowed each territory to decide whether or not it wanted to be a free state or a slave state. Soon, violence broke out in Kansas. Proslavery groups attacked the so-called "free soil" town of Lawrence. When John Brown and his followers struck back in retaliation, the conflict escalated into a wave of chaos and destruction that became known as Bleeding Kansas.

In the fall of 1859, after the Harpers Ferry raid and John Brown's trial and conviction, Virginia governor Henry A. Wise feared that Brown's execution might cause a slave rebellion or that Northern abolitionists would try to rescue Brown. To prevent such a maneuver, Wise requested federal troops. He also called out the VMI cadets and units of the Virginia Militia to keep order. Major Jackson was present at Brown's execution, prepared to use his howitzers if necessary. On December 2, 1859, however, John Brown was hanged without incident.

Like many others, Jackson was alarmed by the hotly contested, razor-sharp issues that were tearing at the fabric of the Union. He hoped that the nation could be held together. The relationship between North and South already had become so tattered and frayed, however, that there was little real hope of repair. War seemed imminent. At the forefront was the topic of states' rights. Since the days of the American Revolution, there had been two schools of thought on this matter. In the South, people believed that each state should have the right to make its own laws, including laws on slavery. According to Southerners, the United States Constitution gave the ultimate source of political authority to the separate states. In contrast, many Northerners favored a strong central government that passed laws for the entire nation. In the North, people wanted the federal government to outlaw slavery in all new territories and states. Although Jackson had strong Union ties, he disagreed with the stance of the Northerners. He felt that the free Northern states were depriving the Southern states of their rights.

Abraham Lincoln was a candidate for president in the election of 1860. Lincoln favored a strong federal government and wanted to stop the spread of slavery. If he became president, Southerners worried, the government also would abolish slavery in the South. South Carolina threatened to secede from the Union if Lincoln won the election. When Lincoln was elected, South Carolina kept its word. By March of 1861, seven Southern states had seceded: South Carolina, Mississippi, Florida, Alabama, Georgia, Louisiana, and Texas. On January 26, the same day that Louisiana left the Union, Jackson wrote a letter to his nephew Thomas Arnold, who had just turned 15. In the letter, as quoted in Farwell's *Stonewall*, Jackson explained why it was crucial for the North and South to make peace.

"People who are anxious to bring on war don't know what they are bargaining for," he wrote. "They don't see all the horrors that must accompany such an event."

On February 1, Texas seceded. A week later, representatives from the seven rebellious Southern states met in Montgomery, Alabama. They adopted a constitution for a new government in a new nation that they called the Confederate States of America. On February 18, Jefferson Davis, an 1824 West Point graduate, was elected president of the new Confederacy. Meanwhile, President Lincoln refused to recognize the Confederacy as a separate government. He insisted that the Southern states still belonged to the Union.

On April 12, 1861, Union troops attempted to resupply Fort Sumter in Charleston Harbor, in Confederate South Carolina. When Union troops refused to give up the fort, Confederate troops opened fire. After three days, the Rebels finally surrendered to the Union soldiers. Although the fight at Fort Sumter was hailed as a victory in the North, Southerners were appalled. After the battle, Virginia, Arkansas, North Carolina, and Tennessee seceded from the Union to join the Confederacy. The bloodiest war in American history had begun. People in western Virginia did not wish to leave the Union, however. This still-loyal territory ultimately was admitted to the Union as the state of West Virginia on June 20, 1863.

With all hopes for peace shattered, Jackson's loyalty was to Virginia. The cadets at VMI received orders to report to Richmond, Virginia, under the command of Major Jackson. Jackson hastily packed his bags and ate a final meal at his home. He then read the fifth chapter of Second Corinthians—a part of the Bible that speaks of the ministry of reconciliation—and prayed with Anna. Throughout the war, Jackson believed that God guided his every step, and he completely surrendered his life to God's will.

At twelve-thirty on the afternoon of April 21, Jackson sat stiffly on his horse as the VMI cadets lined up outside the

The enormous cultural and ideological differences between the North and South prompted a call from several states for secession. Seven Southern states announced the formation of the new Confederacy, a union separate from the recognized government of the United States. Jefferson Davis, a prominent Southern statesman, was voted in as the president of the Confederacy.

barracks.Jackson's orders were to begin the march to Richmond at 1:00. Impatient, some of the young officers shouted, "Let's go! Let's go!" Jackson dismounted and sat down on a nearby stool. "When the clock strikes the hour, we will march, and not until then," he announced in a stern and steady voice. As soon as the deep gong of the clock tower resounded, Jackson remounted. "Right face!" he commanded. "By file left. March!" Row by row, in step, the cadets disappeared over the bridge that spanned the North Branch of the James River. Without looking back, they left behind the nearly empty barracks of VMI. Many of them would never return.

The cadets arrived in Richmond the following day. Jackson marched them to the Hermitage Fair Grounds, a mile and a half outside the city. That evening, at a convention in Richmond, Jackson was promoted to the rank of colonel. The event is recorded in Farwell's *Stonewall*. When the promotion was suggested, one man stood up and said, "Who is this Major Jackson that we are asked to commit him to so responsible a post?" A friend of Jackson's, who was familiar with his bravery in the Mexican War, replied, "He is one who, if you ordered him to hold a post, will never leave it alive to be occupied by the enemy." There were no further arguments. Jackson left at once for Harpers Ferry, where he assumed command of that post.

STONEWALL

At Harpers Ferry, Jackson organized the volunteer companies into battalions or regiments. He also rushed all arms, machinery, and raw materials that had been stockpiled at the arsenal to Richmond. There were few posts as important to the Confederacy as Harpers Ferry. Not only did the town hold the arsenal, but it also was a center for communication between Rebel forces. The Baltimore and Ohio Railroad, the principle line that connected Washington, D.C., with cities to the west, passed directly through town. Also, the busy Chesapeake and Ohio Canal lay just across the Potomac River, on the Maryland shore. Harpers Ferry had become the Confederate headquarters for assembling militia units from miles around. By the time Jackson arrived, on April 29, about 8,000 troops already had gathered there.

At Harpers Ferry, Jackson bought his soon-to-be-famous horse. Little Sorrel was a stocky, barrel-chested workhorse, and Jackson thought the mount, which he originally named Fancy, would make a good horse for Anna after the war. Far from the prancing steed that most commanders rode, Sorrel was a smallish, homely horse. He had strong, broad shoulders, however, and muscular legs.

In early July, Union troops led by General Irvin McDowell began to advance on the Confederate capital of Richmond. Confederate general Pierre G.T. Beauregard, already stationed near Richmond, requested reinforcements. Jackson, in command of the First Brigade of the Confederate Army of the Shenandoah, moved with Brigadier General Joseph E. Johnston, who had replaced Jackson as commander at Harpers Ferry.

McDowell had halted at Centreville, about six miles from the strategic railroad crossing at Manassas Junction. With an army of 30,700 Union soldiers, McDowell should have launched an immediate attack on Beauregard's limited force of 20,000 troops. Such an attack would very likely have brought victory to the Union and could have changed the entire course of the war. McDowell, however, was worried about his inexperienced officers and untrained troops. He hesitated.

On the morning of July 18, Jackson's brigade of 1,500 men began the march to Manassas. Brigadier General Barnard Bee followed with an artillery unit. On July 19, Jackson's brigade reached Manassas. Jackson positioned his men in a pine grove near Mitchell's Ford. Fearing that Union general Robert Patterson would discover that Johnston's army was on the way to Manassas and move his army in to reinforce McDowell, the Confederate commanders decided to make the first attack. At the time, the Rebel troops held strong defensive positions, facing east and northeast along the banks of Bull Run, a tributary of the Potomac. As battlefield commander, Beauregard planned to launch a heavy attack on the Union's left flank. His strategy counted on Johnston's entire Rebel army arriving at Manassas and assumed, too, that McDowell would not move. He was wrong on both counts.

McDowell made the first strike. He attacked the Confederate left flank with his main forces. He then set off on a wide sweep northward as he launched another assault at a stone bridge where the Warrenton Turnpike crossed Bull Run. McDowell's plan would have been a good one if Johnston had failed to show up with a large number of men. The opening shots were fired in the First Battle of Manassas (Bull Run) at eight forty-five on the morning of July 21, 1861.The battle stretched through what became a scorching afternoon. At the outset, Jackson's brigade was positioned on the right of the Confederate line, in support of a brigade under the command of James Longstreet. In another area of the battlefield, Confederate captain John Imboden shouted out in frustration that Bee's brigade had failed to sufficiently protect his guns. At that moment, Jackson's troops marched up through the suffocating smoke and dust. "I'll support your battery," Jackson said to Imboden.

When two fresh batteries arrived to reinforce his brigade, Jackson moved his guns to the front of the line and positioned two regiments behind them. This created a formidable strongpoint. Jackson then placed regiments on both the right and the left sides, among the pines. In the heat of the day, the odors of the battlefield—sweat, blood, and burning powder—mingled with the scent of pine. As Jackson formed his line of battle, wounded soldiers, survivors of collapsing regiments, and retreating men passed through the ranks of his brigade. Panic and fear marked the faces of these fleeing men, and they were an unnerving sight for Jackson's young soldiers. Jackson paced back and forth on Little Sorrel. His chin, tipped skyward, was set and confident. His steady and controlled demeanor earned the admiration of his soldiers and inspired bravery in them.

From his position, Jackson could follow the action as it took place on the battlefield ahead. About noon, Bee galloped over to Jackson and reported that his men were falling back; the enemy soon would be upon him. "Then, sir," Jackson replied, "we will give them the bayonet." Dashing back to rally his men, Bee shouted out, "Look! There is Jackson standing like a stone wall. Let us determine to die here and we will conquer. Follow me!"

The Union launched several gallant charges, but Beauregard managed to stand firm. In the volley of bullets, Jackson's left hand was hit with a musket ball between the palm and the knuckle of his middle finger. The ball broke a bone. Little Sorrel also was shot, but not fatally. Although outgunned, the Confederates maintained order. Beauregard ordered an all-out charge. At that moment, Jackson's calm expression vanished into a look of raw determination. "Charge, men," he called, "and yell like furies!" Whooping and hollering, the men started off in a stampede. They pierced the Union line at the center, but the charge was not enough to break the line.

The battle raged on through the afternoon. By 3:00, it looked as if the Union might win. Beauregard, however, refused to accept defeat. He put Jackson in command of the troops on Henry Hill and ordered another charge. This time, the Union soldiers were thrown back and were dispersed in a chaotic retreat. The Confederate advance came at a high price, however. Both General Bee and Colonel Francis Stebbins Bartow were shot and lay dying.

When the dust settled, a battlefield strewn with mangled bodies came into sharper view. The moans of bleeding soldiers begging for a drink of water floated through the humid air, which was fetid with the stench of death. Union casualties reached 2,600 to 3,000; between 460 and 480 of those casualties were dead. On the Confederate side, of nearly 2,000

Although Jackson was not in favor of war, his devotion to his home state of Virginia had him fighting for the Confederacy. Leading the First Brigade of the Confederate Army of the Shenandoah against the Union *(above)*, Jackson's determination to fight to the death inspired his men and the soldiers surrounding them.

casualties, about 375 were dead. Fighting in the thick of the battle, Jackson's brigade suffered the heaviest tolls: 119 dead and 442 wounded. Jackson walked away from the First Battle of Manassas a legend in the making: His new nickname of "Stonewall" was forever etched in history. Jackson's company became known as the Stonewall Brigade—the only Confederate brigade to have a name. Although highly praised by Beauregard and General Johnston for his fearlessness, Jackson was not heralded as the hero of the day. As commander of the battlefield, that glory belonged to General Beauregard. Just before the battle, however, Jackson had been promoted to brigadier general. Most brigade commanders already held this title, but few were more deserving of it on that bloody afternoon than General Stonewall Jackson.

THE SHENANDOAH VALLEY

When the Civil War began, in April 1861, Jackson was an unknown VMI major. In October 1861, scarcely six months later, he was a newly minted major general in command of an

THE STONEWALL BRIGADE

When Virginia seceded from the Union on April 17, 1861, Governor John Letcher called for militia companies in the Shenandoah Valley to make haste to Harpers Ferry, in order to secure the town and armaments at the arsenal. These 2,611 men were organized into five regiments of infantry and a battery of artillery and designated as the First Brigade, Virginia Volunteers. The Valley men were placed under the command of then colonel Thomas J. Jackson. Jackson, who left his teaching position at the Virginia Military Institute to join the Virginia forces, had been picked by Robert E. Lee, then an adviser to Jefferson Davis.

At the First Manassas (Bull Run), Jackson and the First Virginia Brigade tasted the action of war. Jackson's refusal to move from his position earned him the name "Stonewall," and so his tough brigade became known as the "Stonewall Brigade." The brigade followed Jackson through the Romney campaign in the first winter of the war, which

entire division. Soon, Jackson was placed in charge of the new Department of Northern Virginia and given the task of defending the 150-mile-long Shenandoah Valley. He established camp near Winchester, an important town that controlled crucial turnpikes and a railroad at the northern end of the valley.

Although winter was approaching, and most armies hunkered down during the cold months, Jackson did not want to sit still. First, he attempted to sever the Union's link to coal and other supplies by destroying a dam along the Chesapeake and Ohio Canal. He failed to cut off the supplies, but he locked

solidified the relationship between men and commander. In 1862, the brigade became part of the Valley Army. On their home turf, Jackson led the "Stonewall Brigade" in defeating three separate Union armies. At the same time, the Valley Army kept Union reinforcements away from Richmond—the Confederate capital—during General George McClellan's failed campaign on the Peninsula.

The brigade followed Lee into Maryland and then to Chancellorsville, where their first commander—Jackson— was shot by friendly fire. With a deep, son-to-father love of their general, the men of the Stonewall Brigade were devastated by Jackson's death shortly after Chancellorsville in May of 1863. The brigade pressed on without him, fighting in the Battle of Gettysburg at Culp's Hill. By April of 1865, only 210 men from the original Stonewall Brigade were left at Appomattox. Because of its reputation, the Stonewall Brigade was the first to march through Union lines at the surrender.

Union forces into the area, preventing them from being used elsewhere. Next, he devised a plan to strike Romney, a Union stronghold about 40 miles west of Winchester. Near the end of the year, he led 10,000 troops on an expedition to attack Romney that started in good weather. By nightfall of the first day, however, Jackson's soldiers were besieged by snow and ice. They managed to capture the town of Bath in West Virginia, but in a sloppy attack. The troops moved on, with the icy wind slicing through their uniforms and blankets. Jackson was more concerned about the feet of his horses than the fate of his freezing men. By the time the march stopped, the sick and exhausted soldiers were cursing him under their breath. Thankfully, the 18,000 Union troops stationed at Romney had fled the city when they heard about Jackson's planned attack. There was no battle. Leaving 4,000 soldiers at Romney to guard the city, Jackson led the Stonewall Brigade and the rest of his troops back across the mountains to the warmth of Winchester.

The soldiers who stayed in Romney had not been trained by Jackson. They were under the command of General William Loring, a veteran who had lost an arm in the Mexican War. Winter at Romney was a terrible experience. Men fell sick, and the disheartened soldiers began to blame the man they thought had abandoned them—Stonewall Jackson. Senior officers wrote letters of protest to members of the Confederate Congress. Loring signed the letter and agreed that Jackson's entire winter campaign had been poorly planned and executed. Loring believed that Jackson had bruised the morale of his fine soldiers. When Jackson received Loring's letter, he noted his disapproval on it. He then forwarded the message to Richmond, confident that the matter would be dismissed. Much to Jackson's surprise, the letter generated much attention. It traveled all the way to the Confederate secretary of war, Judah Benjamin, and to President Jefferson Davis. Hearing only one side of the story, Davis and Benjamin ordered Jackson to pull the discontented troops out of Romney.

On January 31, 1862, Jackson obeyed the order. On the same day, he sent in his resignation and expressed his displeasure with the whole Romney ordeal. Jackson wanted to resume teaching at VMI. He believed that he would be of greater use there, especially if there was going to be such interference with his command. General Johnston was stunned. There was no way he was about to let the hero of Bull Run slip away. Johnston finally convinced Jackson to withdraw his resignation. Seeking vindication, Jackson brought court-martial charges against Loring. The Confederate officials dismissed them, however.

Meanwhile, on the war's Western Front, the Union had established the upper hand. The Confederacy was vulnerable in the west because of its many waterways, which were exploited by the Union's superior navy. The Union's fleet of ironclad ships prowled the broad and twisting rivers of the Mississippi Valley as Union general Ulysses S. Grant waged a successful land campaign. The Union had captured Nashville, Tennessee, on June 6, 1862. In the following months, Northern gunboats and infantry also conquered New Orleans, the South's major port and largest city.

The Eastern Front still belonged to the Confederacy, however. This was thanks, in part, to the Union's overly cautious military tactics in the region. In March 1862, General Johnston—outnumbered four to one—pulled his Confederate troops back to within just six miles of Richmond as legions of Union soldiers landed around Yorktown, Virginia. At this point, a swift Union blow likely would bring the Confederate Army to its knees. The Union's General George B. McClellan seriously overestimated the size of the Confederate forces at Richmond, however. Johnston was holding on with a small army of only 13,000 men, but McClellan believed that there were about 100,000 soldiers in Johnston's force. Instead of launching an attack, McClellan set up camp and waited for Washington to send more men. Johnston could hardly believe his luck. The delay allowed Confederate reinforcements to arrive in time to defend Richmond.

In the faraway Shenandoah Valley, Stonewall Jackson was getting ready to unleash a summer rampage that would brand his name in history books and strike fear in the hearts of Northerners. The Yankees dispatched a large force that would have been strong enough to defeat Jackson if it had been led by someone other than Major General Nathaniel Banks, a former Massachusetts governor and congressman who lacked military experience. Banks moved his army of 35,000 men across the Potomac in early March to occupy Harpers Ferry and the surrounding area. His next target would be Winchester, where Jackson was stationed with just 5,000 Confederate troops. With Banks's sizeable army breathing down his neck, Jackson decided to pull out of Winchester and spring a surprise attack on his Union pursuers.

On March 11, 1862, Jackson ordered his commanding officers to place wagons and men on the road that led out of town. This movement would draw Union forces into the area and give them a sense of control. After nightfall, by the light of a full moon, Jackson planned to swing around and strike his unsuspecting enemy in a rare nighttime attack. His senior officers misunderstood Jackson's somewhat imprecise directions, however, and moved the wagons and men too far south to make the necessary spin around. Jackson lost his opportunity to assault an unprepared enemy.

On the road out of Winchester, Jackson grumbled about his officers' blunder. "That is the last council of war I will ever hold!" he said, as quoted in Stonewall Jackson, by Donald Davis. Jackson vowed to keep his future plans to himself rather than trust subordinates. He once said that if his hat knew his plans, he'd burn it. For the rest of the war, he stayed true to his vow.

During the next week, Jackson retreated further into the Shenandoah Valley. He paused briefly at Strasburg, 18 miles from Winchester, and finally stopped at Mount Jackson, almost 25 miles from Strasburg. General Banks was chasing Jackson with a beefed-up division commanded by Brigadier General James Shields and was confident that he had Jackson on the run. The Union generals lost track of Jackson, however. Although Jackson was settling into a defensive position at the mountain, Shields assumed that Jackson must have abandoned the valley and gone to join the Confederate forces at Richmond. Agreeing, Banks ordered Shields to pull all the way back to Winchester. Banks prepared to return to Washington, satisfied with his apparent success. To Jackson, this opportunity was too good to pass up. He lunged out of his defensive position to become the hunter instead of the hunted.

Jackson led his army back to Strasburg. There, he learned that Union regiments already were passing through Winchester on their way to Harpers Ferry. In a grueling pursuit, Jackson pushed his soldiers to continue marching. Just outside the village of Kernstown, south of Winchester, Union soldiers spotted the advancing Confederates. To seek a fight when so outnumbered was practically unheard of. Shields almost refused to believe his soldiers' report. He had to ride back and see the advance for himself. When Shields appeared on a ridge, a round of Rebel artillery shells blew him right off his horse. Although severely wounded, he survived. Further Union reconnaissance parties found only some Confederate cavalry in the area. Both Shields and Banks agreed that Jackson would not start a battle without more men.

At first, Jackson planned to attack the following morning. He changed his mind, however, because he believed that any delay might give the Union commanders time to recover from their surprise and reinforce their brigades. The Confederates, Jackson now knew, must attack immediately. After an exhausting day of marching, his soldiers would have to dig deep into their stores of grit and courage to find the strength for battle. Jackson rallied them to fight.

Swinging his brigades eastward, Jackson found Union soldiers already formed into lines and prepared to wage battle. The hope of surprise vanished. One of Jackson's aides galloped out to a high point and surveyed the field below. Endless lines of blue uniforms marched forward. The aide hurried back to tell Jackson how outnumbered the Confederates would be. Jackson ordered the man to keep quiet. A furious battle soon erupted and wore on, mercilessly, for hours.

On the field, Jackson tried to cause confusion in the Union lines. He barked out orders one after another and threw himself into the heat of battle. Finally, when their ammunition was completely gone, the Stonewall Brigade cracked. General Richard Garnett ordered them to fall back. This triggered a full-scale retreat. Jackson's best men—his very own Stonewall Brigade—had broken in the face of the enemy. They did not stand firm and fight with bayonets. The Confederates managed to hold back the Union forces long enough to make a clean retreat. Shields and Banks, still convinced that only a madman would fight such a one-sided battle, settled into defensive positions. The Confederates did the same. Enraged, Jackson relieved Garnett as commander of the Stonewall Brigade and had him arrested.

Jackson's army suffered a bitter defeat that day, at what became known as the Battle of Kernstown. Jackson lost about one-third of his troops, with 80 dead, 455 wounded, and more than 260 missing. In a hasty retreat, the Confederate soldiers were forced to leave behind some of their wounded. Anna Jackson's brother was among those who were captured. Many of the soldiers probably thought that the battle was a foolish idea. After watching Jackson unleash his wrath on Garnett, however, no officer would dare to disobey the general.

Nicknamed the "Pathfinder," General John C. Frémont was told to direct his troops toward Shenandoah Valley, Virginia, in order to cut off Jackson's retreat route. The Union, however, underestimated Jackson's military prowess and the Stonewall Brigade defeated Frémont's forces (*depicted above*).

Jackson's bold move to chase General Shields alarmed the federal government and threw the whole Union strategy off kilter. Suddenly, Union commanders saw the Shenandoah Valley as a broad path that could carry the Confederate Army all the way to Washington. In a rash moment, President Lincoln shifted his focus from capturing Richmond to protecting the capital against this new menace named Stonewall Jackson. After Kernstown, Banks turned his 25,000 Union troops back to the valley. The division at Harpers Ferry was put on high alert. Lincoln also ordered General McDowell to keep 35,000 men around Manassas to fortify the Union defenses around Washington instead of moving additional troops to Richmond.

Seldom in history had one small battle created such havoc among the victors. Stonewall Jackson's defeat delivered a blow as stunning as if he had won.

In the first week of April, Jackson established his position in an area known as Rude's Hill. This secure refuge offered access to the Valley Turnpike, which ran along the western edge of the Massanutten Mountains and provided paths through the enemy line of the Shenandoah Valley and into the neighboring Luray Valley. The only entry point for the enemy was a single bridge over the North Fork of the Shenandoah River. If forced to retreat, Jackson would be able to fall back through the mountain passes and reach the safety of General Johnston's army at Richmond. Another 8,000 Confederate soldiers were nearby, under the command of Major General Richard Ewell, a West Point graduate and veteran of the Mexican War.

On April 17, a Union cavalry captured the North Fork bridge. This opened the gate to Jackson's position at Rude's Hill. Jackson's Valley Army was forced to retreat. As Jackson plodded along on Little Sorrel, his gaze became lost in deep thought. In his mind, he painted a tactical military masterpiece, one that he soon would play out. Although the Union forces might have thought that he was running to Richmond, he had other plans. He moved eastward and tucked into another secure position in the Elk Run Valley. Once again, Shields lost sight of Jackson's army and jumped the gun. He reported to Washington that Jackson had retreated to Richmond. By the end of April, thousands of federal troops were pulled out from deep in the Shenandoah Valley, both to reinforce the Union armies in the west and to offer more troops to McClellan.

During this time, Jackson kept in close contact with General Robert E. Lee, who served as a military adviser to President Jefferson Davis. General Johnston acted as overall field commander of the Confederate Army. Lee agreed with Jackson's idea to dart away from Washington and strike in western Virginia, in an attempt to throw the Union Army there off balance. Jackson would go after John "Pathfinder" Frémont, who commanded more than 15,000 Union soldiers spread throughout the rugged mountains and valleys of western Virginia.

Before dawn on April 30, 1862, Jackson's Valley Army of 6,000 men, reinforced by Ewell's division, marched out of Elk Run on its way west. This time, Jackson told no one of his plans, at least not more than was absolutely necessary. Almost as soon as the men began marching, the sky opened up and pelted them with heavy downpours. After a two-and-a-half days' slog through muck and mud, the army reached Port Republic, only 16 miles southwest of Elk Run.

Jackson's first target was the town of Front Royal. It was located at the junction of the two forks of the Shenandoah River, at the head of the Luray Valley. This was the southeastern point of a strategic triangle and, as far as Jackson was concerned, a weak link. The next point of the triangle was Strasburg, to the northwest, across the Shenandoah's North Fork. The uppermost point was Winchester, to the northeast. The recovery of Winchester would clear the Confederates' way to Harpers Ferry and, from there, across the Potomac River to Washington. By this time, Jackson's army had been reinforced to 17,000 veteran soldiers and more than 40 artillery pieces, which were hidden by the bulk of the Massanutten Mountains.

The Union force at Front Royal was commanded by Colonel John Kenly. At two in the afternoon of May 22, the Confederates pounced on the 1,000 Union soldiers protecting the town. The Rebels severed the Yankees' communication lines so that General Banks could not be alerted. As Kenly fled, he torched his camp and rushed toward the bridges over the Shenandoah with the hope of burning them behind him. Confederate forces quickly secured the South Fork bridge, however, and saved the North Fork bridge by tossing Kenly's burning hay bales over the sides. The road to Winchester was still open. Confederate cavalrymen chased after the Union soldiers and captured 750 of them. By nightfall, Front Royal was isolated.

Those Union soldiers who managed to escape delivered the dreadful news to Banks. Immediately, he began to abandon his positions. By first light, the road out of Winchester was clogged with federal wagons and troops. Meanwhile, Jackson moved his units ahead, not to hit Strasburg, but, rather, to strike at the Valley Turnpike, nine miles south of Winchester. When he got there, he knew he would find Banks's wagon train, slogging along. At once, Jackson's blue eyes blazed with intensity. Taking a couple of brigades with him, he crossed over the rough countryside to head off the Union column.

By the time Jackson's force reached the turnpike, the front of Banks's column had already passed, but a slow and steady river of blue uniforms continued in front of him. The Confederates opened fire, practically at point-blank range. They blew wide gaps through the panicking Union line. At the same time, Confederate cavalry stormed vulnerable sections of the Yankee column. Before long, the scene became one of carnage and destruction.

Hungry for more, Jackson pushed his soldiers even harder. They headed northeast toward Winchester, over bloody corpses, fallen horses, and strewn weapons and supplies. Time was an enemy, and Jackson did not want to give his Union foes a chance to regroup. Although some of his weary troops collapsed at the side of the road, Jackson pressed on. The next morning, as the battle raged once again, he spread his remaining units around Winchester. Mounted on Little Sorrel and pacing the front lines, Jackson sat erect and composed, his stern orders punctuated by the crack of gunfire. When the Union line at last gave way, he shouted, "Forward! After the enemy!" Roused by the promise of victory, the Stonewall Brigade found a new surge of strength. With wild cries, the Rebel soldiers charged after the fleeing Yankees.

Now this pesky general who was supposed to have been crushed by Union forces weeks before was standing just across the Potomac River, with his sights set on Washington. President Lincoln moved quickly to trap Jackson. He called up new militias to help defend Washington. He also ordered Frémont to abandon his drive in Tennessee and, instead, move in on Jackson. General McDowell was to press in from the east to join Frémont behind the Confederate line. Banks would reenter the Shenandoah Valley from the northeast. A total of 60,000 Union troops were set to the task of stopping Stonewall Jackson.

As soon as Jackson found out that these Union generals were on the move, he knew that he had to pull out, and quickly. On the rainy morning of May 30, 1862, his eight-mile-long wagon train was on the move. With the Union Army closing in, Jackson's retreating army was in real danger. Once again, his men had to endure a grueling march. The Stonewall Brigade was familiar with hardship, however, and his men had learned to trust "Old Jack." Through drive and determination, Jackson's men reached Strasburg before the Union forces. The Confederates made a narrow escape with Union troops only a few miles away.

The final battle in the Shenandoah Valley took place at Port Republic on Monday, June 9. It was a fierce fight and pivoted back and forth throughout the day. During the battle, Jackson, who had been running too long without sleep, collapsed on a bed and fell asleep, fully dressed. A short time later, an officer entered the room and awoke him. Jackson immediately got back to work, but his lack of sleep caused him to make a dangerous mistake. Confederate infantry units were still taking their positions when the Rebels discovered that Jackson had overlooked a small, high plateau that was a perfect location for big guns. Capitalizing on Jackson's oversight, the Union forces already had placed artillery on the plateau.

After hours of brutal fighting during which the Union came close to victory, the Confederates captured the plateau guns in a frantic bayonet charge and took over the strategic high ground. With the captured artillery pieces trained on their former owners, the battle tipped to the Confederacy. Having defeated both Frémont and Shields in separate battles (Frémont's army had been pushed back the day before), Jackson at last pulled back. When the last echo of the last bullet had fallen silent, he led his men across the bridge into Port Republic, and they burned the bridge behind him.

At Richmond, General Johnston decided to take advantage of the distraction caused by Jackson's latest venture. He decided to launch his own attack on McClellan, who still was waiting for his reinforcements. The battle, which became known as Seven Pines, took place in a swampy area. Johnston's timing was right, but the weather was not. Mucky roads and bad luck kept entire Confederate units from the battlefield. Neither side gained any ground, but the Battle of Seven Pines set the stage for an important turning point in the war. During the battle, Johnston was wounded. With Johnston no longer able to command, Jefferson Davis appointed Lee the new battlefield commander. To the front of the Confederate forces stepped a perfectly matched, stunningly powerful military duo: Stonewall Jackson and Robert E. Lee.

Seven Days

Stonewall Jackson was to meet with General Lee at Confederate headquarters in Richmond on Monday, June 23, 1863, to discuss strategy. Not wanting to disobey the Sabbath by engaging in any activity that was not focused on God, Jackson refused to leave Gordonsville, Virginia, where he had arrived with infantrymen, until after midnight. He rode through the night and finally galloped into Richmond, about 65 miles away, at three on Monday afternoon.

In his plan to defeat McClellan, Lee decided to split his army. At Richmond, 25,000 Confederate troops would continue to guard the earthworks, keeping McClellan in place. Lee and 65,000 Confederate soldiers would move against Union commander Fitz-John Porter's 30,000 men. Stonewall Jackson's unit would attack Porter's right flank. Once Jackson launched

General Robert E. Lee, the commander of the Confederate Army, was a formidable opponent to any military officer drafted by President Abraham Lincoln. With similar military careers and experiences, Jackson and Lee were frequently in contact with each other and provided each other with battle advice. They last met before the Battle of Chancellorsville *(above)* at a generals' conference on strategy.

his attack, A.P. Hill would hit Mechanicsville, thereby endangering Porter's rear flank. When A.P. Hill moved south, General Longstreet and Daniel Harvey Hill, Jackson's West Point comrade and brother-in-law, also would strike. These multiple attacks would force Porter to pull out of his position. On paper, the strategy looked foolproof, but the attack was complex, and timing was critical.

Initially, the attack was planned for the morning of Thursday, June 26. As the sun set on Monday, Jackson galloped out of Richmond on an all-night ride. He pounded along rain-washed roads to the Beaver Dam Station, 40 miles away, and arrived at daybreak. Having gone two days without sleep, he collapsed in front of a roaring fire, his muddy boots still on his feet. After a short nap, he spent the day moving columns of men and wagons through the drizzle along sloppy roadways. By nightfall on Tuesday, the troops had advanced an incredible 20 miles in horrible conditions. With only 27 hours left before the battle, however, Jackson's men still had another 25 miles to go. On Wednesday, the sun had dipped beneath the horizon by the time the Confederate soldiers reached Ashland, six miles from the attack's designated starting point. With the assault scheduled to begin in just a few hours, there was no way that Jackson's men could be there in time.

Reluctantly, Jackson informed Lee that he was not ready to launch the attack. He halted with his men so that they could eat a hot meal and rest. Jackson, however, had no sleep. He stayed up all night preparing and woke his men at three in the morning to resume the march.

Meanwhile, General McClellan made an unexpected attack on Wednesday night at Oak Grove, near the Seven Pines battlefield. At first, he planned to make a major advance, but he had second thoughts when the initial scuffle turned into a heated battle. This engagement, which was the first fight in a week of battles that came to be known as the Seven Days, had no effect on Lee or on the Confederates' northern line, where Jackson still was slogging along.

On Thursday, confusion struck the Confederate forces. Jackson's men still had not reached their position. The route they were following was littered with fallen trees and destroyed bridges, which delayed their progress. Although he was six hours behind schedule at 9:00 in the morning, Jackson still hoped to wage battle that day. He sent a message to Brigadier General Lawrence O'Bryan Branch to move out and notify A.P. Hill. Branch led his brigade across the Chickahominy River at the town of Half Sink and turned toward Mechanicsville. For some reason, however, the message never reached Hill.

Noon passed, and then the early afternoon hours, and still no one had heard from Jackson except Branch. At 3:00, Hill decided that he could wait no longer. Although he had received no orders from Lee, he believed that the plan was in serious jeopardy. He unleashed his 16,000 soldiers on Mechanicsville. Porter retreated a mile and hung along the sharp ridges of Beaver Dam Creek, a narrow waterway with steep banks draped in thick brush. Hoping to pry the Yankees out, Hill's troops charged into a ferocious battle—the very event that Lee had wanted to avoid.

Jackson's men finally reached the area around 5:00 in the afternoon. McClellan soon learned that Jackson was nearby, waiting, like a cougar, to pounce. That day's battle had not included the Valley Army. McClellan imagined how bloody the fight might become if Stonewall's brigade joined it. Although the Confederates were losing miserably, McClellan ordered Porter to abandon his strong positions at Beaver Creek Dam and pull back. Jackson's fearsome reputation alone had spooked the enemy.

On Friday, the third morning of the Seven Days, A.P. Hill informed Jackson that Union soldiers now were positioned around Gaines' Mill, on Powhite Creek. Later that afternoon, Lee pulled Jackson aside for a private conversation. Lee painted a picture of the day's events. A.P. Hill was to attack Porter in the center as Longstreet hit the Union's left flank. Jackson was to take a position on the other side of A.P. Hill. Daniel Harvey Hill would circle behind Jackson to extend the Confederate line. Jackson spoke to some cavalrymen who knew the area and could serve as guides. He instructed them to point his army toward Cold Harbor, unaware that there were two Cold Harbors in the area. One was Old Cold Harbor; the other was New Cold Harbor. The one that Jackson needed to find was Old Cold Harbor, but his vague description prompted his guides to move toward New Cold Harbor. When Jackson heard the thunder of cannons in the opposite direction, he realized his error. He was several miles southwest of where he needed to be.

Part of the reason for Jackson's blunders was his debilitating exhaustion. He had gone for months without proper rest. Grogginess had eaten away at his sharp mind. Amazingly, he was remarkably healthy in other respects, especially considering his chronic health problems and the fact that he had been marching through some of the worst weather conditions he had ever encountered. War seemed to transform Jackson's physical and emotional state, and he was untouched by weakness. He finally had reached his breaking point, however.

Jackson showed up at the battlefield and pulled his men into position. Lee greeted the tardy Jackson with a friendly handshake. "Ah, General, I am glad to see you!" Lee said. "I had hoped to be with you before!" Lee's mild irritation was short-lived, however. He continued without hesitation, "That fire is very heavy. Do you think your men can stand it?"

After having fought a harsh battle all day, the Union soldiers were spent. McClellan had another 60,000 troops within reach, but he refused to send them to Porter despite receiving that very advice from other generals. Porter clung to the high ground along the edge of the creek and toppled wave after wave of Rebel attackers. Then Confederate colonel John B. Hood and his brigade of tough Texans broke through the center of the Union line. Porter retreated to join the rest of McClellan's huge, but idle, force.

Lee and his commanders had won a decisive victory. It came at a high price, however. At least 8,750 Confederate soldiers were dead, wounded, or captured. Union losses numbered 6,837 men.

McClellan moved his base to the James River to add naval support. Lee tried to intercept McClellan's army in the battles of Savage's Station, on June 29, and Frayser's Farm, on June 30, but was unsuccessful. Then, McClellan posted his army on

Malvern Hill, a strong defensive position on the bank of the James River, 18 miles southeast of Richmond. On July 1, in the Battle of Malvern Hill, Union troops repeatedly threw back Confederate attacks during some of the most brutal fighting of the war. The next day, however, McClellan declined to take the offensive. Instead, he withdrew to Harrison's Landing. As hard as he tried, Lee failed to tear apart McClellan's retreating army. Nevertheless, Lee saved Richmond. Union forces did not get as close to the Confederate capital again until 1864.

SECOND BULL RUN

After the Battle of Cedar Mountain on August 9, Jackson met with Lee at Gordonsville for a council of war. Jackson informed Lee that General John Pope was camped about 20 miles away and was vulnerable. Thousands of Union troops had crossed the Rappahannock but not the Rapidan, and were sandwiched between the two rivers. The Confederates were positioned in front of the Yankees, and this left only a single bridge over the Rappahannock over which Pope could possibly escape. Lee took this opportunity to attack.

Lee's strategy unfolded like a game of chess. The Confederates moved to cross the Rappahannock in late August. Jackson's old Stonewall Brigade, under the command of William Taliaferro, led the way north and west. The brigade followed along the banks of the river as Union soldiers matched it step for step on the other side. Along the way, Jackson spotted a crossing point. It was near Sulphur Springs, and no Union troops were on the opposite bank. Acting quickly, Jackson sent infantry brigades and artillery pieces across. Well after this transport was under way, a torrential storm rolled in, causing the Rappahannock to rise six feet. The Confederate troops were stranded on the Yankee side of the river, with raging water separating them from the rest of Jackson's army. Jackson was furious about the sudden rain. It took nearly two days for his soldiers to build a makeshift bridge to retrieve the isolated troops.

Meanwhile, Confederate J.E.B. ("Jeb") Stuart made a spectacular cavalry raid behind Union lines. He plundered General Pope's headquarters, barely evading capture. In addition to grabbing $250,000 of federal money, he snatched confidential papers detailing communications between Pope and Lincoln.

Back on the Rappahannock, the Rebels continued to move along, side by side with Pope. The stalemate was more than Lee could stand. He made a bold decision to split his army, despite the fact that the Union forces greatly outnumbered his. At night on August 25, as lingering Confederate forces staged fake movements, Jackson and his division moved out. Despite the summer heat, Jackson's army of 23,000 soldiers marched swiftly. They traveled 26 miles on the first day.

Pope had 75,000 men on hand and more on the way. Lee had a total of 55,000 soldiers, but had just sent half of them off. Just as Lee hoped, Pope misread the situation and overestimated the size of the Confederate forces. Pope assumed that Jackson was heading back to the Shenandoah Valley. If this were the case, Pope figured, Lee must have enough men to feel safe about sending Jackson away.

Once again, Jackson kept his own plans so secret that even his divisional commanders did not know where they were headed. Once his army had disappeared behind the low-lying Bull Run Mountains, Jackson suddenly turned east and pushed quickly toward the Union rear. By late afternoon on August 26, Jackson's men had passed through Haymarket and Gainesville and stood alongside the Alexandria-Warrenton Turnpike. At this point, Stuart galloped in with his cavalry to reinforce Jackson. Moving toward Manassas Junction, Jackson came to a fork in the road. He sent Ewell's division down the left road to capture the railroad town of Bristoe.

The rest of the Rebels captured Manassas. They discovered that the junction town had been transformed into a huge Union supply depot. Storehouses and railroad cars brimmed with all sorts of supplies, including ammunition, artillery pieces, uniforms, blankets, cigars, and food. It looked like Christmas to the Confederate forces that day. Soldiers gorged themselves on bacon and canned lobster and sipped mugs of coffee, brandy, and whiskey. This success gave a tremendous boost to Jackson's ego. He had led his troops on an amazing 54-mile sweep around the right flank of the Union Army without being detected.

On August 27, Pope responded to Jackson's bold maneuvers. Union regiments, shuttled in by train from Washington, marched straight for Manassas Junction and straight into a waiting line of Confederate artillery. With a hint of arrogance, Jackson personally rode out to ask for a Union surrender. A smattering of Yankee bullets flew toward him, and his Confederate troops unleashed a powerful strike in response. At the same time, Pope launched a counterstrike: He forced Ewell out of Bristoe. When Pope turned to hit Jackson, however, he lost track of the overall strategic setup. Happily for Lee and Jackson, Pope had taken the bait. Lee and Longstreet were only 20 miles away and closing in fast.

In midafternoon, Jackson calmly trotted out of Manassas with two wagon trains of captured supplies. Confederate soldiers stuffed as much loot as they could into their pockets and belts. Whatever was left behind they set ablaze. The sky over Manassas erupted with flames, smoke, and sparks, accompanied by a series of booming explosions. By midnight, the Confederate Army had assembled along a ridge near Groveton. From their camp, the men could hear the rushing waters of Bull Run as it ran beneath the stone bridge of the Warrenton Turnpike. Jackson sat on his loyal Little Sorrel and gazed down on the old Bull Run battlefield, the place where he first became "Stonewall."

With the railroad junctions at Manassas and Bristoe destroyed, the turnpike seemed to be Pope's last line of retreat. Jackson stood in position right beside him, however. A spur line of the Manassas Gap Railroad was under construction. The section was being built to leave the main trunk line at Gainesville, run across Bull Run, and follow the turnpike. As

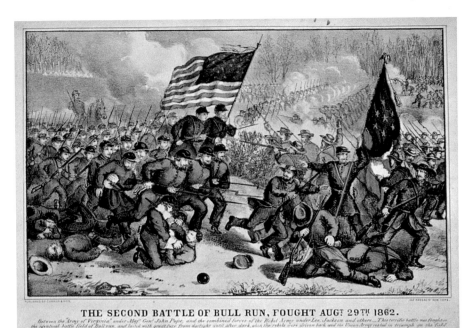

THE SECOND BATTLE OF BULL RUN, FOUGHT AUG? 29TH 1862.

Between the "Army of Virginia" under Maj: Gen! John Pope, and the combined forces of the Rebel Army under Lee, Jackson and others. This terrific battle was fought on the identical battle field of Bull run, and lasted with great loss from daylight until after dark, when the rebels were driven back, and the Union Army rested in triumph on the field.

The Second Battle of Manassas, or the Second Bull Run *(above)*, was an exciting victory for the Confederacy. Outnumbered by about 20,000 men and having dismissed even more men in a psychological maneuver, Jackson successfully led his regiment into a secret military offensive against the Union.

part of the as-yet incomplete construction, a deep and long gouge had been dug out for the tracks. This ditch gave Jackson's men a ready-made defensive spot. As Pope's men maneuvered in the blistering sun, Jackson's soldiers rested in shade, out of enemy sight.

Jackson built a superb combined-arms defense of infantry, artillery, and cavalry. His line stretched for about two miles: A.P. Hill's division was on the left, near Sudley Springs; Ewell's men were at the center; Taliaferro and the Stonewall Brigade were on the right. Behind this line, on the high ground of Stony Ridge, Jackson had dug in the Rebel artillery.

Late in the afternoon of August 29, Jackson's army unleashed a sudden attack on an exposed Union flank. An incredible slaughter followed; it continued until both sides were practically face-to-face and still firing. The battle lasted for two-and-a-half hours, with the Confederate line holding on. Two of Jackson's three divisional commanders were hit in the cross-fire. Taliaferro suffered multiple wounds; General Ewell was shot in the left knee and lost his leg. Pope was under the illusion that the battle was a Union success. He now knew exactly where Jackson's position was, and he planned to strike the Confederates with all that he had. Jackson knew that he had to hold out only until Lee and Longstreet arrived.

By dawn, the largest force of Union troops was concentrated to the east, in front of A.P. Hill's division. The actual fight began on the west, however, on the far right end of Jackson's line. During the artillery duel, Jackson crouched among his pounding big guns. All around the Confederate line, enemy cannon-balls ripped through the trees and tore up the ground. Then, suddenly, the Confederate soldiers heard the welcome sound of Rebel yells growing louder and louder. Reinforcements had arrived. It was General John B. Hood's steely Texans, one of the best fighting brigades in the Confederate Army. With the arrival of Hood's men, Jackson knew that his right flank was safe.

On the Confederate left, however, the battle was another story. For the rest of the day, Hill and his men fought for their lives. They managed to throw off the Yankees' brutal assaults, but the constant charges rattled the Rebel line. Each time the Union soldiers fell back, the Confederates stripped the dead of any usable ammunition. At one point, Jackson rode over to see for himself how Hill was holding up. As recounted in *Stonewall Jackson,* when he found Hill, he said, "General, your men have done nobly. If you are attacked again you will beat the enemy back." As Jackson spoke, new volleys of musket fire shrieked through the air. "Here it comes," hollered Hill. As Jackson galloped away, he called back, "I'll expect you to beat them!"

Finally, late in the afternoon, Hill's troops forced the Yankees back and broke the final charge of the day. As soon as

Jackson heard the news, he smiled and said, "I knew he could do it." After six hours of ferocious fighting, not an inch of ground had been gained.

As the sun rose the next morning, the battlefield was quiet. The silence must have been eerie after the previous day's deafening crossfire. Lee and Longstreet had arrived the day before and were ready to join the contest. At 3:00 in the afternoon, a single cannon shot sparked the battle. Nearly 10,000 Union soldiers moved against Jackson, leaving the Union's left flank totally exposed. Astonished, Lee opened fire with his big guns to blast jagged holes in the Union flank. Longstreet's troops charged in, and the Union line collapsed in a chain reaction that rippled across the entire front. Lee's army then pivoted toward Hill's army at Sudley Springs and swept over the hazy field, plowing eastward toward the stone bridge. Pope ordered a retreat and made a final stand on Henry House Hill at about 6:00 in the evening. The defeated Union Army staggered wearily over the stone bridge.

THE BLOODIEST DAY

On September 13, 1862, General Lee's Order 191 was discovered by a Union private in a field of clover outside Frederick, Maryland. The order was in an envelope and wrapped around three cigars. The document detailed Confederate plans: Three separate columns, totaling almost 23,000 men, were to march on Harpers Ferry, surround the place, and capture or destroy the Union garrison there. Afterwards, Lee's entire army was to reassemble at Boonsboro, Maryland, 20 miles north of Harpers Ferry.

As soon as McClellan got his hands on the information, he set out to dismantle the Confederate Army. For once, he knew where the Confederates were and exactly where they were going.

The information could have proved fatal for the Confederacy. A Southern sympathizer alerted Lee in time for him to change his plans, however. On September 15, 1862, Jackson won a brilliant and tactical victory at Harpers Ferry in just 90 minutes. He then left A.P. Hill behind to sort out the surrender details and took off with his army on another midnight march; General Lee was calling.

Sharpsburg was a rectangular village that sat on both sides of the Boonsboro Road, a route that ran east to west and passed over the twisting Antietam Creek. This waterway marked the front line for the opposing armies. The Rebel line already was established. General Longstreet was set up on the creek beneath the town, with the left of his line ending about a mile up the Hagerstown Turnpike. D.H. Hill had spread his men in front of the place where Longstreet and Jackson would link; his left flank was guarded by Jeb Stuart's cavalry all the way to the Potomac. Artillery batteries were positioned on the Nicodemus Hill to the north, where a small, forested area known as the North Woods provided a natural barrier against advancing troops. Across the turnpike, Rebel soldiers crouched down among the tall cornstalks of David Miller's field. More artillery dotted the area behind the West Woods, which overlooked the field. Another strongpoint was secured in the house of a local farmer, in the surrounding buildings, and along the farmer's fence. By 3:00 in the afternoon on September 16, Jackson had about 7,700 men in position.

At 6:00 the following morning, September 17, Union general Joseph "Fighting Joe" Hooker kicked off the bloodiest day in the Civil War. An overnight rain had left a lingering ground fog so thick that Jackson's men could not see the enemy. Union cannon exploded with a rumbling roar on the cornfield as the insistent pop and shrill of musket fire echoed for miles. Union infantrymen blazed through the cornfield, slashing at the Rebels hiding there. Before long, the corn was cut down to the roots. As the fog cleared, more Union soldiers emerged from the North Woods in long, precise lines of bright blue, the sunlight bouncing off their bayonets. They had pulverized the

Confederate position in the cornfield; now, they made a steady sweep toward the farmhouse. The Rebels fought back with fiery determination, but they were pushed back and forced out of both the East and West woods.

As Union troops pushed toward the Hagerstown Turnpike, they disturbed the hearty breakfast of Hood's Texans. Like hornets from a nest, the rowdy Confederate brigades opened fire and charged the Yankees with a terrifying Rebel yell. Eventually, the Union attack crumbled; the Yankees dropped back along the turnpike and the cornfield, both of which were blanketed by the dead. Fighting Joe Hooker, who was wounded, lost almost half of his 8,800 men.

Once again, Stonewall Jackson lived up to his name. As soldier after soldier crumpled to the ground, he showed no fear. He rode through his batteries, directing their fire and encouraging his men. Later, he told a friend that on no other day of battle had he ever felt so calm. He was certain that God would protect him from all harm.

Believing that the Confederate line must have been weakened by the repeated assaults, McClellan threw what he thought would be the final punch. He sent out a corps of 6,000 men, who advanced in lines 500 yards long. Meeting little opposition, the soldiers did not properly protect their flanks. They swept straight into a curved spot in the Confederate line in a movement that exposed the Union flanks and rear. The unexpected crossfire pounded the Yankees so badly that the woods looked as if they were on fire. Within just a few minutes, 2,355 Union soldiers lay dead or wounded. Those who remained bolted in fear, chased by Rebels for half a mile.

At this point, McClellan shifted his attention to the Confederate right flank and the bridge at Antietam Creek. He handed the task of capturing the bridge to Major General Ambrose E. Burnside. If Burnside could take the bridge, the Union soldiers could cross and attack at Sharpsburg. Instead of employing all four of his divisions at once, however, Burnside

Jackson led his men into battle at Antietam *(above)*, the bloodiest conflict of the Civil War. Although there were many casualties, more than in any other battle during the war, the fighting ended in a draw.

funneled them onto the narrow bridge one division at a time. They proved to be easy picking for a brigade of 400 Georgia soldiers. The Confederates held the bridge for more than three hours, but at about one in the afternoon, the Yankees finally captured it. The way into Sharpsburg was wide open.

Just when it seemed as if the Union would win, however, Burnside made a critical mistake. The battle for the bridge had taken too long. Burnside then squandered two hours just getting his men over the creek and into position for the advance. It was Jackson's late-arriving division that saved the day. A.P. Hill had finally wrapped things up in Harpers Ferry and arrived at Sharpsburg just as the sunlight started to dim. His men pitched into Burnside's exposed flank and drove him up a hill near the bridge. It was there that the bloody Battle of Antietam drew its final breath. In just a single day of fighting, there was a combined total of 23,000 casualties. The Union Army suffered 2,108 killed, 9,549 wounded, and 753 captured or missing. On the Rebel side,

1,512 were dead, 7,816 lay wounded, and 1,844 were captured or missing. More American soldiers were killed or wounded at the Battle of Antietam than died in the Revolutionary War, the War of 1812, the Mexican War, and the as-yet-to-be-fought Spanish-American War combined.

Not long after the battle at Antietam, Jackson received some uplifting news. From time to time throughout the war, Jackson managed to spend short visits with his dear wife, Anna. On November 23, 1862, Anna gave birth to a baby girl in Charlotte, North Carolina. This time, both mother and child were healthy. Undoubtedly, Jackson wished that he could have been there. Anna's sister Harriet took one look at the blue-eyed, dark-haired, eight-and-a-half-pound Julia and said that she was the image of her darling papa. Although Jackson had hoped for a son, he wrote to Anna and told her to make sure that his daughter knew that "he loves her better than all the baby boys in the world." Anna promised to send him a lock of Julia's hair at Christmas.

On the last Sunday in November, Stonewall Jackson rode into the empty city of Fredericksburg, Virginia. Neither he nor Lee wanted to fight there, but the Union Army was advancing toward Fredericksburg on its way to Richmond. What turned out to be one of the most one-sided battles of the Civil War took place at Fredericksburg on December 13, after Union forces had occupied the city. The Union suffered a crushing defeat, with 1,284 soldiers killed, 9,600 wounded, and 1,769 captured or missing. The Confederates had 608 dead, 4,116 wounded, and 653 captured or missing.

With the slaughter of Antietam still an open wound, President Lincoln stabbed at the South where he knew it would hurt the most. On January 1, 1863, he issued the Emancipation Proclamation, which freed all slaves in the Rebel states. The war was no longer about preserving the Union; now, it was about bringing freedom to all Americans.

"Let Us Cross Over the River"

With the bloody year of 1862 coming to a close, Stonewall Jackson settled into winter quarters on the grounds of a mansion known as Moss Neck, about 12 miles below Fredericksburg. The place was owned by Richard Corbin, a planter who served as a private in Jackson's army. Corbin and his wife urged Jackson to stay in the main house, but the general declined, not wanting to infringe on the family's privacy. Instead, he stayed in a two-story hunting lodge about 500 yards from the house.

For the time being, the fighting had stopped. After Fredericksburg, both armies dug in along the banks of the Rappahannock and watched each other shiver in the cold. During this time, Jackson became terribly homesick. Sometimes, senior officers got their troops settled into camp

While Jackson was away on the front line of battle, his wife, Anna, gave birth to their daughter, Julia *(above)*. Like many other soldiers, Jackson had not seen his wife for a long time and would often write letters in an effort to dispel his homesickness.

for the cold months and then took leave to go home. Jackson, however, remained at his post. He often wrote letters of longing to Anna. "I haven't seen my wife for nearly a year—my home in nearly two years," he wrote in one letter, as quoted in Davis's *Stonewall Jackson*, "and have never seen our darling little daughter." When he received the lock of Julia's hair at Christmas, he wrote, "How I do want to see that precious baby."

Trying to fill the emptiness he felt in his heart, Jackson asked the Corbins' six-year-old daughter, Janie, to come and play in his office each afternoon. Little Janie became his favorite visitor. Jackson often presented her with gifts, once even snipping a piece of gold lace off his hat and handing it to her.

In March of 1863, Jackson shifted his headquarters from Moss Neck to Hamilton's Crossing, six miles south of Fredericksburg. He traded his comfortable lodge for a canvas tent. It was here that Jackson received the heartbreaking news that Janie Corbin, his surrogate daughter, had died of scarlet fever. The stonelike general wept without shame and decided that he must see his family. On April 20, Anna and five-month-old Julia arrived by train at Guinea Station, five miles from Hamilton's Crossing. At the station, Jackson climbed into the train car and met his daughter for the first time. He then took his wife and daughter by covered carriage to the plantation home of William Yerby, where he had arranged for temporary lodging. Each day, he hurried back from Hamilton's Crossing to see his wife and play with his rosy-faced baby. Swinging little Julia in front of the mirror, he'd say, "Now, Miss Jackson, look at yourself! Isn't she a little *gem?*"

Meanwhile, across the Rappahannock, Fighting Joe Hooker had built his Army of the Potomac to about 135,000 men. Hooker did not want to repeat the mistake that Burnside made at Fredericksburg: the disastrous failure of a series of frontal attacks against entrenched Confederate positions. The key points at which to spearhead a defeat of the Confederates, Hooker believed, were at the river crossings northwest of Richmond. To accomplish his goal, Hooker copied one of Lee's maneuvers and divided his immense army. In the opening phase of his plan, a new cavalry corps of 10,000 troopers would sneak out of the camp, ride far beyond the Confederate left flank, and cross the Rappahannock. These troopers then would swoop back to raid supply depots and destroy communication routes between Lee and Richmond. Once the cavalry began to disrupt things behind Rebel lines, another 50,000 Union soldiers would attack the entrenchments at Fredericksburg, thereby holding Lee in place. The bulk of Hooker's army then could move out to the northwest, cross the Rappahannock, and wheel back southward. This move would force Lee out of his Fredericksburg fortress to fight in the open.

Hooker's plan was ingenious. He did not take Virginia's unpredictable springtime weather into consideration, however. Additionally, no matter how clever he was, he still had to face Robert E. Lee and Stonewall Jackson. Just as Hooker's plans got under way, torrential rains pounded the area and caused the Rappahannock to swell. For two weeks, Hooker's 10,000 cavalrymen were stranded as they waited for the river to sub-side. After the two weeks of unrelentingly foul weather, Hooker decided to go ahead with the rest of his plan; he would let the cavalry join in when it could.

Hooker threw his main punch: He unleashed three infantry units to head for Kelly's Ford, 25 miles to the northwest. To speed things up, he sent along 2,000 sure-footed pack mules instead of slower-moving wagons to carry the necessary sup-plies over the muddy terrain. Union troops crossed the ford on April 29. Then, splitting their columns for easier movement, the infantry headed to the southeast, toward the Confederate stronghold at Fredericksburg. As the men moved along, how-ever, they encountered more fords. This further divided the Union troops.

The powerful Union right wing reunited in an area of tangled swamps and dense scrub oak known as the Wilderness. Five roads met at the heart of the Wilderness, at a place called Chancellorsville. This strategic crossroads consisted of a large farmhouse and several outbuildings. Here, Hooker established his Union headquarters. Once his troops were concentrated, Hooker galloped in on his tall white horse to taunt the enemy to come out and fight.

Lee and Jackson had no thoughts of dodging this battle. When someone suggested retreat, Jackson barked, "No, sir, we have not a thought of retreat. We shall defeat them." The two generals spent the night of April 30 riding along the ridge behind Fredericksburg to examine the Yankee positions. At last, Lee decided, once again, to split his army of 54,000 men. He planned to leave behind a force of 10,000 in Fredericksburg to face five times as many Union soldiers. The rest of the Confederate troops would follow Lee into the Wilderness.

Jackson pulled the Second Corps in from the south to begin the greatest march of his career. His men moved out long before dawn on May 1, taking advantage of the morning mist that hid them from Yankee spotters. Unwisely, Hooker delayed his attack; it was Jackson who instigated the fight, at 10:30. Jackson advanced with confidence, as if the Confederate forces outnumbered those of the Union, and the battle of Chancellorsville exploded with terrible ferocity. After two hours of intense battle, neither side had broken.

Fighting Joe Hooker was the first to flinch. Afraid that some of his units might be surrounded, he ordered his men to retreat to their original positions. Hooker's decision shocked his commanders, who were reluctant to surrender hard-won ground. As fighting drew to an end for the day, Lee and Jackson planned their next move.

Jackson's mapmaker discovered a road used by woodsmen. The route was about 10 miles long and was wide enough for horses, wagons, and artillery to pass even as it was hidden from view within the woods. Running southwest, the road connected to the Plank Road, a route that wrapped around the exposed Union flank. Although Lee's force already was divided, he took the risk of dividing it again. Lee stayed put with just 14,000 men to face Hooker's 50,000, while Jackson led the remaining 28,000 soldiers and 112 cannons to hit the end of the Union line.

At the end of the lumberjacks' road, Jackson pivoted and twisted sharply northward for one of the most dangerous of all military maneuvers. He marched his 28,000 men across the front of the enemy force while keeping an eye on his own flank. Jackson knew that speed was crucial. He rode among his men, urging them to hurry. The Confederate force reached the front of the Union line at two in the afternoon on May 2. The Yankee unit was facing in the opposite direction from that of Jackson's approach, and the 900 Union soldiers already had stacked their weapons and begun to fix their evening meal.

By sunset, Jackson had moved 18,500 men and the majority of his artillery into position. He glanced at his pocket watch; it was just after five. Jackson gave the signal to attack, and the Rebels surged into the Wilderness, throwing the unsuspecting Yankees into panic.

Meanwhile, General Hooker stood on the porch of the Union headquarters at Chancellorsville. As soon as he realized that his soldiers were under attack, however, he mounted his horse and led a fresh division of troops toward the battle site. Growing darkness brought confusion to both sides, but Jackson refused to quit. This fight offered the kind of action that excited him: rattling the enemy with a surprise attack and then pursuing them to the bitter end. In the chaos, however, Jackson was hit three times and seriously wounded.

One bullet had punctured the palm of his right hand, breaking several small bones. More serious, however, was a wound to his left arm: The bullet had sliced through his arm from elbow to wrist. A third musket ball had shattered the bone just below his left shoulder, breaking his arm and severing an artery. Bleeding heavily, Jackson had to be carried off the battlefield in an ambulance wagon. The battle raged on without him and ended with Fighting Joe's retreat across the

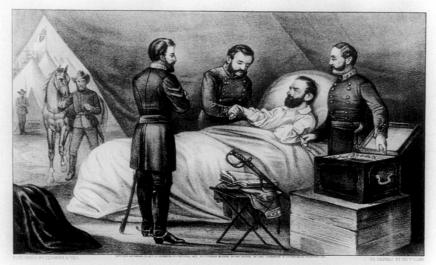

THE DEATH OF "STONEWALL" JACKSON.

In an unfortunate incident, Jackson lost his left arm when his own men mistakenly shot at him. Jackson survived the amputation, but unfortunately contracted a fatal case of pneumonia and later died in a military hospital. The general who led the Confederate forces to so many glorious victories is remembered today throughout the South as one of the greatest military figures in history.

Rappahannock. Against the worst of odds, Jackson had masterfully orchestrated another Confederate victory. His thirst to dismember the enemy led to his downfall, however. Ironically, the shots that felled Stonewall Jackson came, by mistake, from one of his own men.

The wounded general was taken to Guinea Station to rest and recover, with the hope that he would be back in command soon. Jackson's left arm was so severely mangled that it had to be amputated. His wounds began to heal, however, and he planned to return to active duty as soon as he was fully recovered. Lee was devastated by the loss, even if temporary, of his best general. "He has lost his left arm," he lamented, "but I have lost my right arm."

Jackson did not recover. He developed pneumonia and fell seriously ill. At times, because of his high fever, he was delirious; he shouted out battlefield orders as he tossed restlessly in bed. On Sunday, May 10, Jackson could feel the hand of death reaching for him. Showing the same bravery that he showed in battle, he was not afraid to die. "It is the Lord's Day; my wish is fulfilled," he said. "I have always desired to die on a Sunday."

Shortly after 3:00 in the afternoon, Jackson said his good-byes to Anna and little Julia, who sat by his side. With his final breath, he whispered, "Let us cross over the river and rest under the shade of the trees." The mighty Thomas "Stonewall" Jackson died at 3:15 in the afternoon on May 10, 1863. He was 39 years old. On May 15, his body returned home to Lexington, Virginia, for his final resting place.

THE CONFEDERACY FALLS

Through the years, people have wondered how the Civil War might have turned out if Stonewall Jackson had lived. As it happened, the South eventually toppled to the Union's superior manpower and resources. On April 9, 1865, General Robert E. Lee surrendered to General Ulysses S. Grant at Appomattox Courthouse in Virginia. With or without Jackson, the Confederacy probably was doomed from the beginning. It is better, perhaps, that Stonewall Jackson did not live to experience that defeat.

 CHRONOLOGY

1824   Thomas Jonathan Jackson is born in Clarksburg, Virginia, to Jonathan and Julia Jackson.

1826   Jackson's father and sister Elizabeth die of typhoid fever.

1831   Mother Julia dies of complications during childbirth on December 4; Jackson goes to live with his uncle Cummins Jackson at Jackson's Mill.

1846   Jackson graduates from West Point. The Mexican War begins.

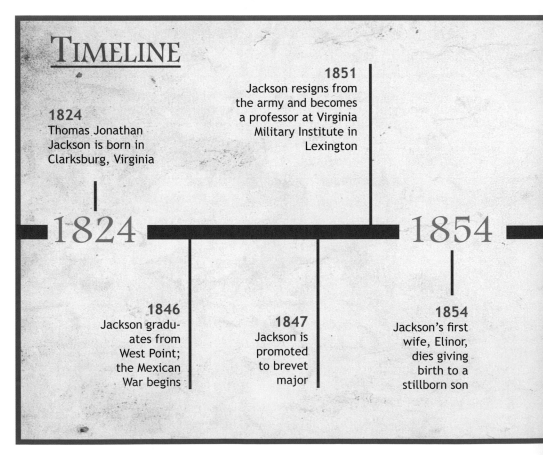

TIMELINE

1824
Thomas Jonathan Jackson is born in Clarksburg, Virginia

1851
Jackson resigns from the army and becomes a professor at Virginia Military Institute in Lexington

1824

1854

1846
Jackson graduates from West Point; the Mexican War begins

1847
Jackson is promoted to brevet major

1854
Jackson's first wife, Elinor, dies giving birth to a stillborn son

1847 Jackson establishes himself as a brave officer in the battle for Mexico City; by war's end, he is promoted to brevet major.

1851 Jackson resigns from the army and becomes a professor at Virginia Military Institute in Lexington.

1853 Jackson marries Elinor Junkin on August 4.

1854 Elinor dies giving birth to a stillborn son on October 22.

1856 Jackson tours Europe during the summer.

1857 Jackson marries Mary Anna Morrison on July 16.

1857
Jackson marries Mary Anna Morrison

1863
Jackson makes the greatest march of his career at the Battle of Chancellorsville and launches a surprise attack on Union forces; Jackson is shot during crossfire and dies of pneumonia on May 10, at age 39

1857 — 1865

1861
Civil War begins. Jackson is put in command at Harpers Ferry and earns the name Stonewall. He is promoted to major general of the Valley Army. He wins several battles for the Confederacy

1865
The Civil War ends

1861   **April 12** Confederate troops open fire on Union troops at Fort Sumter, South Carolina, and the Civil War begins; Jackson is put in command at Harpers Ferry.

July 21 The Battle of First Manassas (Bull Run) takes place; Jackson earns the name "Stonewall" and his unit becomes the "Stonewall Brigade."

October Jackson is promoted to major general of the Valley Army.

May–June Jackson orchestrates the amazing Shenandoah Valley Campaign, with victories at Front Royal, Winchester, Cross Keys, and Port Republic; after this success, he is ordered to join General Robert E. Lee in eastern Virginia, on the Peninsula, against General McClellan.

June 15–July 1 The Seven Days battles are fought, and lack of sleep causes Jackson to make mistakes.

August 9 Jackson wins the Battle of Cedar Mountain; there are Confederate victories at the battles of Second Manassas (August 29) and Antietam (September 17).

November 23 Daughter Julia Laura is born.

December Jackson settles into his winter headquarters at Moss Neck in December.

1863   **May 1** The Battle of Chancellorsville begins; on the second day of the battle, Jackson makes the greatest march of his career and launches a surprise attack on Union forces; during the crossfire, Jackson is hit by three .57-caliber bullets from the rifle of one of his own men.

May 10 Jackson dies of pneumonia on May 10, at age 39.

1865　**April 9** Confederate general Robert E. Lee surrenders to Union general Ulysses S. Grant at Appomattox Courthouse; the Civil War ends.

GLOSSARY

abolish   To end.

abolitionist   Someone who opposes slavery and works to end it.

annex   To add to something larger.

artillery   Mounted guns, such as howitzers and other cannon.

battalion   A tactical military unit that forms part of a division.

beachhead   A position gained by invading an enemy shore.

big guns   Heavy artillery, such as cannon.

bombardment   An attack with artillery.

caisson   A two-wheeled wagon with a chest for ammunition.

campaign   A series of military operations designed to reach a single goal.

casualties   Those who are wounded, killed, or captured in a battle.

causeway   A raised path or road.

commissary   An army officer in charge of supplies.

court martial   A court where a person is tried who is accused of a military crime.

demerit   A mark against a student for poor conduct or poor grades.

earthworks   Embankments or fortifications made by piling up dirt.

entrench   To surround with ditches, or trenches.

flank   The left or right side of a military formation.

formidable   Difficult to approach or attack.

garrison   A military post or station.

hazing   Forcing someone to do ridiculous things as part of an initiation, as at a school.

howitzer   A short cannon.

infantry   Foot soldiers.

ironclad   In the Civil War, a ship covered with iron plating for protection.

light artillery   Small-caliber howitzers and cannon.

limber   A two-wheeled vehicle to which a gun is attached.

parade   An organized march for display.

plebe   A military trainee; at West Point, a first-year student.

rank   In the military, a certain position.

reconnaissance   A search of an area to seek out information about an enemy position.

regiment   A military unit smaller than a division.

reveille   A signal on a bugle or drum in the morning to wake soldiers.

salvo   The discharge of a number of guns at once.

secede   To withdraw.

tattoo   A signal on a drum or bugle to alert soldiers that it is time for bed.

 BIBLIOGRAPHY

Bowers, John. *Stonewall Jackson: Portrait of a Solider*. New York: William Morrow and Company, 1989.

Davis, Burke. *They Called Him Stonewall*. New York: The Fairfax Press, 1988.

Davis, Donald. *Stonewall Jackson*. New York: Palgrave MacMillan, 2007.

Farwell, Byron. *Stonewall*. New York: W.W. Norton & Company, 1992.

Krick, Robert. *Stonewall Jackson at Cedar Mountain*. Chapel Hill: The University of North Carolina Press, 1990.

Robertson, James I., Jr. *Stonewall Jackson: the Man, the Soldier, the Legend*. New York: Macmillan Publishing, 1997.

Royster, Charles. *The Destructive War: William Tecumseh Sherman, Stonewall Jackson, and the Americans*. New York: Alfred A. Knopf, 1991.

Warriors: Stonewall Jackson. A&E Biography, 1995.

FURTHER RESOURCES

Aretha, David. *Jefferson Davis*. New York: Chelsea House Publishers, 2009.

Crompton, Samuel Willard. *Ulysses S. Grant*. New York: Chelsea House Publishers, 2009.

Hyslop, Steve. *Eyewitness to the Civil War*. Washington, D.C.: National Geographic, 2006.

Koestler-Grack, Rachel A. *Abraham Lincoln*. New York: Chelsea House Publishers, 2009.

———. *William Tecumseh Sherman*. New York: Chelsea House Publishers, 2009.

Malaspina, Ann. *Harriet Tubman*. New York: Chelsea House Publishers, 2009.

McNeese, Tim. *Robert E. Lee*. New York: Chelsea House Publishers, 2009.

Potter, Bill, and Stephen Lang. *Beloved Bride: The Letters of Stonewall Jackson to His Wife*. San Antonio: Vision Forum, 2002.

Ray, Delia. *Behind the Blue & Gray: The Soldier's Life in the Civil War*. New York: Lodestar Books, 1991.

Robertson, James. *Stonewall Jackson's Book of Maxims*. Nashville, Tenn.: Cumberland House, 2002.

Sonneborn, Liz. *Harriet Beecher Stowe*. New York: Chelsea House Publishers, 2009.

Sterngass, Jon. *Frederick Douglass*. New York: Chelsea House Publishers, 2009.

———. *John Brown*. New York: Chelsea House Publishers, 2009.

WEB SITES

The American Civil War
www.theamericancivilwar.com

Detailed site about the people, places, and events that made up the Civil War.

CivilWar.com: The Home of the Civil War
www.civilwar.com

Official records, battle maps, and the largest collection of Civil War photos online.

The Civil War: A Film by Ken Burns at PBS
www.pbs.org/civilwar

Information about the film by Ken Burns, historical documents, and a section for educators to use in classrooms.

The Stonewall Brigade
www.stonewallbrigade.com

Award-winning site for the living history association, which is dedicated to providing accurate information about soldiers who served in the Civil War.

Stonewall Jackson House, Lexington, Virginia
www.stonewalljackson.org

A source of information about the life and times of Jackson, particularly his days in Lexington.

PICTURE CREDITS

PAGE

9: © The Virginia Military Institute Archives

12: The Bridgeman Art Library

17: © The Virginia Military Institute Archives

25: The Granger Collection, New York

30: © Courtesy of the Library of Congress, [3b51010u]

36: © The Virginia Military Institute Archives

41: © Courtesy of the Library of Congress, [3b50709u]

45: Getty Images

51: The Bridgeman Art Library

56: © The Virginia Military Institute Archives

60: © The Virginia Military Institute Archives

64: © The Virginia Military Institute Archives

69: © The Virginia Military Institute Archives

74: The Granger Collection, New York

80: The Bridgeman Art Library

85: Getty Images

93: Getty Images

100: Getty Images

107: © Courtesy of the Library of Congress, [3b50865u]

112: © Bettmann/Corbis

115: © The Virginia Military Institute Archives

120: © Courtesy of the Library of Congress, [3b35218u]

INDEX

A

Antietam, Battle of, 109–113
Arista, Mariano, 35
Arnold, Laura Ann (born Jackson) (sister), 15–16, 55, 65, 66, 70
Arnold, Thomas Jackson (nephew), 70, 78

B

Banks, Nathaniel, 8, 10, 90–93, 96
Barney, Lowry, 58–59
Bartow, Francis Stebbins, 84
Beauregard, Pierre G.T., 82, 84, 85–86
Bee, Barnard E., 30, 82–84
Benjamin, Judah, 88–89
Big Hill (Cerro Gordo), Battle of, 41–44
Bowers, John, 18
Branch, Lawrence O'Bryan, 101–102
Bravo, Nicolas, 50
Brown, John, 72–75, 77–78
Bull Run (Manassas), First Battle of, 82–86
Bull Run (Manassas), Second Battle of, 104–109
Burnside, Ambrose E., 111–112
Butcher, Gibson, 19–20, 27

C

Camp Spencer, 23–24
Cedar Mountain, Battle of, 8–11
Chancellorsville, Battle of, 87, 116–120
Chapultepec, Battle of, 50–53
Churubusco, Battle of, 47, 49
Civil War, beginning of, 75–81

Civil War, end of, 121
Civil War battles. *See specific battles by name*
Clay, Henry, 76
Company E, First Artillery, 57
Company G, First Artillery, 43–46
Company I, First Regiment, 44–46
Company K, First Artillery, 33, 35–43, 42, 55–56
Confederate States of America, 79
Contreras, Battle of, 47–49
Corbin, Janie, 116
Corbin, Richard, 114–116
Cortez, Hernando, 38

D

Davis, Jefferson, 79, 86, 88–89, 94, 98

E

Emancipation Proclamation, 113
Ewell, Richard, 8, 94, 105–108

F

"flying artillery," 44
Fort Columbus, 33, 35
Fort Hamilton, 35, 55–57
Fort Meade, 57–58
Fort Polk, 38
Fort Putnam, 29
Fort Royal, 95–96
Fort Sumter, 79
Fredericksburg, Battle of, 113
Frémont, John C. "Pathfinder," 95, 97–98
French, William Henry, 58
Fugitive Slave Act, 77

G

Garnett, Richard, 92
Gilham, William, 60
Gordon, George H., 51
Grant, Ulysses S., 21, 28, 30, 35, 89, 121

H

Hardee, William Joseph, 61
Harpers Ferry, Virginia, 72–75, 81–82, 90, 109–110
Harris, Thomas A., 60–61
Hays, Samuel Lewis, 18–20
Hill, A.P. (Ambrose Powell), 8, 30, 100–102, 107–108, 110, 112
Hill, Daniel Harvey, 63–65, 100, 102, 110
Hill, Isabella, 63–65, 68
Hood, John B., 103, 108
Hooker, Joseph "Fighting Joe," 110, 116–119
Houghton, Marie, 58
Houghton, Roland, 58

I

Imboden, John, 83

J

Jackson, Andrew, 24
Jackson, Anna (Mary Anna, born Morisson) (wife), 68–71, 82, 113, 115, 116, 121
Jackson, Cummins (uncle), 15, 19–20, 31, 55
Jackson, Edward (grandfather), 15
Jackson, Elinor (Ellie, born Junkin) (wife), 63–67
Jackson, Elizabeth (great-grandmother, born Cummins), 14
Jackson, Elizabeth (sister), 15, 67
Jackson, George Washington, 19
Jackson, John (great-grandfather), 14–15

Jackson, Jonathan (father), 14, 15
Jackson, Julia (born Neale, later Woodson) (mother), 14, 15–16, 67
Jackson, Julia (daughter), 113, 116, 121
Jackson, Laura Ann (later Arnold) (sister), 15–16, 55, 65, 66, 70
Jackson, Mary Graham (daughter), 69–70
Jackson, Thomas Jonathan ("Stonewall")
  as businessman, 71
  as cadet (See West Point)
  childhood and family, 14–16
  European vacation, 67–68
  youth at Jackson's Mill, VA, 16–18
  health and illnesses, 57, 58–59, 70
  marriages, 63–67, 68–70
  religion and, 57, 66–67, 79
  resignation submitted and withdrawn, 89
  slaves owned by, 70–71
  as teacher (See Virginia Military Institute)
  death of, 120–121
Jackson, Warren (brother), 15–16
Jackson, Wirt (half brother), 15
Jackson's Mill, Virginia, 16–18, 67
Jalapa, Mexico, 42–43
Jefferson, Thomas, 20
Johnston, Joseph E., 48, 82, 85, 89, 94, 98
Junkin, Elinor (Ellie, later Jackson) (wife), 63–67
Junkin, George, 63, 65
Junkin, Julia, 63
Junkin, Margaret (Maggie), 63–67

K

Kansas-Nebraska Act, 77
Kenly, John, 95

Kernstown, Battle of, 91–94
Kester, Conrad, 17–18
Kosciuszko, Thaddeus, 20

L
Lee, Robert E.
  appointed battlefield com-
    mander, 98
  Chancellorsville and, 116–118
  at Harpers Ferry, 73
  Jackson and, 8, 86, 94, 99
  Mexican War and, 47
  Second Bull Run and, 104–109
  Seven Days battles and, 101–
    104
  surrender by, 121
  West Point and, 21
Letcher, John, 86
Lexington, Virginia
  household and business in,
    70–71
  marriage to Anna, 68–70
  marriage to Ellie, 63–67
  Virginia Military Institute, 58,
    59–63
Lincoln, Abraham, 7, 78, 79, 93,
  97, 105, 113
Little Sorrel (horse), 10, 82
Lobos Island, 39
Longstreet, James, 30, 83, 100,
  106, 108–110
Loring, William, 88, 89
Louisiana Purchase, 75–76

M
Magruder, John B., 44–46, 48–49,
  52–54
Malvern Hill, Battle of, 103–104
Manassas (Bull Run), First Battle
  of, 82–86
Manassas (Bull Run), Second
  Battle of, 104–109
maxims, 32
McClellan, George B.
  Antietam and, 109
  Jackson and, 99
  Mexican War and, 47

Seven Days, 101–104
  at Seven Pines, 98
  at Shenandoah Valley, 87,
    89–90, 94
  West Point and, 23, 26
McDowell, Irvin, 82–83, 93, 97
McKinley, William, 31–33
Mexican War
  background, 34–35
  Big Hill (Cerro Gordo), Battle
    of, 41–44
  Chapultepec and Mexico City,
    49–53
  Company G, First Artillery,
    43–46
  Company I, First Regiment,
    44–46
  Company K, First Artillery, 33,
    35–43, 42
  Contreras and Churubusco,
    47–49
  end of, 53–54
  land acquired in, 76–77
  San Augustin, 46–47
  Veracruz, seige of, 39–41
  West Point cadets and, 31
Mexico City, fall of, 53
Miller, David, 110
Missouri Compromise, 76–77
Monterrey, Mexico, 37
Morrison, Eugenia, 70
Morrison, Harriet, 113
Morrison, Mary Anna (later
  Jackson) (wife), 68–71, 82, 113,
  116, 121
Morrison, Robert Hall, 68, 70
Moss Neck, 114–116

N
Neale, Julia (later Jackson, then
  Woodson) (mother), 14, 15–16,
  67
Niagara Falls, 65–66, 69

O
150th Virginia Militia Regiment,
  31–33

P

Patterson, Robert, 82
Pillow, Gideon J., 46, 47–48, 54
Polk, James K., 35
Pope, John, 7–8, 104, 105–108
Port Republic, 97–98
Porter, Fritz-John, 99–100, 102, 103

Q

Quitman, John A., 46

R

religion, 57, 66–67, 79
Romney campaign, 86–87, 88–89
Rosecrans, William S., 30
Rude's Hill, 94

S

Saltillo, Mexico, 37–39
San Augustin, Mexico, 46
Santa Anna, Antonio López de, 41–42, 46–47, 49–50
Scott, Winfield, 38–39, 40, 42–44, 46–47, 49–50, 52–53, 58, 61
Seven Days battles, 99–104
Seven Pines, Battle of, 98
Seymour, Truman, 45–46
Shenandoah Valley campaign, 86–98
Sherman, William T., 21
Shields, James, 91–93, 98
slaves, 70–71, 75, 77
Spencer, John Canfield, 21–22
states' rights, 78
Stonewall Brigade, 11, 85, 86–87, 92
Strasburg, Virginia, 91, 95–96
Stuart, J.E.B. ("Jeb"), 105, 110

T

Talbott, Colonel, 17–18
Taliaferro, William, 10, 104, 108

Tallmadge, James, 76
Taylor, Francis, 33, 35, 37–39, 43
Taylor, Zachary, 35, 37–38, 40
Thayer, Sylvanus, 20–21
Treaty of Guadalupe Hidalgo, 53–54
Turnley, Parmenas, 27
Twiggs, David E. "Old Davey," 42, 46, 48

V

Veracruz, seige of, 39–41
Virginia Military Institute (VMI), Lexington, 58, 59–63, 77, 79–81

W

Walker, James A., 62–63
Washington, George, 20, 73
West Point, U.S. Military Academy at
    application to, 18–22
    Camp Spencer, 23–24
    character and social life at, 28–30
    classes at, 24–28
    graduation, 30–31
    history of, 20–21
    Jackson's maxims at, 32
    Mexican War and class of 1846, 31
Winchester, Virginia, 90–91, 95–96
Winder, Charles Sidney, 8, 10
Winder, John H., 43
Wise, Henry A., 77–78
Withers, Alexander Scott, 18
Woodson, Blake, 15–16
Woodson, Julia. *See* Jackson, Julia
Worth, William J., 42, 46, 52, 54

Y

Yerby, William, 116

ABOUT THE AUTHOR

RACHEL A. KOESTLER-GRACK has worked on nonfiction books as an editor and writer since 1999. During her career, she has dealt with historical topics that range from the Middle Ages, to America's colonial era, to the years of the civil rights movement. In addition, she has written numerous biographies of a variety of historical and contemporary figures. She lives with her husband and daughter in the German community of New Ulm, Minnesota.